Fun and Fundamental
MATH
for YOUNG
CHILDREN

*Building a Strong Foundation
in PreK–Grade 2*

Also by Marian Small

Good Questions:
Great Ways to Differentiate
Mathematics Instruction in the
Standards-Based Classroom
(3rd edition)

Teaching Mathematical Thinking:
Tasks and Questions to Strengthen
Practices and Processes

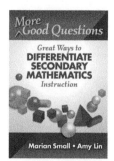

More Good Questions:
Great Ways to Differentiate
Secondary Mathematics Instruction
(with Amy Lin)

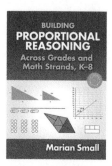

Building Proportional Reasoning
Across Grades and
Math Strands, K–8

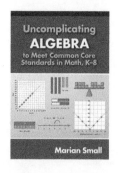

Uncomplicating Algebra
to Meet Common Core
Standards in Math, K–8

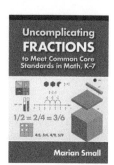

Uncomplicating Fractions
to Meet Common Core
Standards in Math, K–7

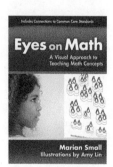

Eyes on Math:
A Visual Approach to
Teaching Math Concepts
(Illustrations by Amy Lin)

Fun and Fundamental
MATH
for YOUNG
CHILDREN

*Building a Strong Foundation
in PreK–Grade 2*

Marian Small

Foreword by Graham Fletcher

TEACHERS COLLEGE PRESS

TEACHERS COLLEGE | COLUMBIA UNIVERSITY
NEW YORK AND LONDON

Ru'bĭcon

Published simultaneously by Teachers College Press, 1234 Amsterdam Avenue, New York, NY 10027, and by Rubicon Publishing Inc., 2040 Speers Road, Oakville, Ontario L6L 2X8, Canada, www.rubiconpublishing.com

Text Design: Lynne Frost
Images: Cartoons and photos, Shutterstock.com; Rubik's cube (p. 178), dnd_project / Shutterstock.com; line art, Lynne Frost
Cover Photo: FamVeld / iStock by Getty Images

Library of Congress Cataloging-in-Publication Data

Names: Small, Marian, author.
Title: Fun and fundamental math for young children : building a strong
    foundation through play in PreK–grade 2 / Marian Small.
Description: New York, NY : Teachers College Press, 2018. | Includes
    bibliographical references and index.
Identifiers: LCCN 2017057736 (print) | LCCN 2018004108 (ebook) |
    ISBN 9780807776964 (ebook) | ISBN 9780807759110 (pbk. : alk. paper)
Subjects: LCSH: Mathematics—Study and teaching (Early childhood)—
    Activity programs.
Classification: LCC QA135.6 (ebook) | LCC QA135.6 .S5648 2018 (print) |
    DDC 372.7/049—dc23
LC record available at https://lccn.loc.gov/2017057736

ISBN 978-0-8077-5911-0 (paper)
ISBN 978-0-8077-7696-4 (ebook)

Printed on acid-free paper
Manufactured in the United States of America

26 25 24 23 22 21 19 18   8 7 6 5 4 3 2 1

Contents

Foreword

EACH FALL, preschool and primary teachers across the United States welcome students from all walks of life into their classrooms with open arms. These teachers are charged with one of the most, if not *the* most, important job in the world: educating and preparing young children for the future. They work tirelessly as they look to build trust, relationships, and a foundational understanding upon which all future learning will stand.

Being married to a kindergarten teacher, I can attest to the countless hours primary grade educators spend outside of the regular school day and throughout the summer months in search of lessons and resources. Rarely does the time allocated for planning within a school day end up being just that. It is usually spent taking their class to and from specials, using the restroom (often the only opportunity in a 7-hour span), or calling a parent for a change of clothes or a forgotten lunch. All of this goes to say that teachers very seldom have the time to invest in their own development and to prepare for what they love—teaching.

Unlike their secondary colleagues, primary teachers on a daily basis prepare for multiple lessons across multiple subject areas. It is for this reason that many preK–2 teachers do not consider themselves as *math teachers,* but more as generalists. There is no doubt that every primary teacher wants to know and understand as much about elementary mathematics as possible. In my experience, teachers are continually seeking knowledge that helps them engage their students in the fundamentals of learning math while still making it fun along the way. But after years in the classroom, where should they turn and what resources can they trust? At a time when math resources are plentiful, it can be tough to choose one resource over another. Teachers face the constant question, "Where will I get the most return for the little time I have to invest?"

Thankfully, Marian Small has once again shared a beautiful blend of pedagogy and practice. Only this time she's written a book specifically for preschool through 2nd-grade teachers. Within the first few pages it quickly becomes apparent that, whether you are a new or a veteran teacher, your knowledge and appreciation *of* and *for* primary mathematics will grow page by page. For years, Small has shared her classroom experiences and empowered K–12 teachers across the globe. As you read this book, you will feel charged with a greater understanding of what primary grade students need to know on their way to becoming successful mathematicians and how to help make it happen.

At the heart of the book is something that Small has continually helped me improve in my own practice over the years: building student autonomy and listening to their thinking. Each chapter begins with the fundamental understandings that teachers should have in order to move student understanding along the trajectory of learning. The nuances and misconceptions that are often missed or overlooked in our classrooms are uncovered—Small does a brilliant job making some of the most difficult concepts accessible.

Each chapter is purposefully laid out to tackle some of the biggest ideas for our youngest learners. From subitizing and rote counting, to addition and subtraction with 2-digit numbers, to measurement and geometry, Small explains the importance of each concept and then provides practical and fun tasks that get 4-, 5-, 6-, and 7-year-old boys and girls engaged in key mathematical ideas. Each task shared throughout the book is carefully designed to provide students of all abilities with opportunities to make inferences and conjectures, ideas often missing in a primary classroom.

If you are familiar with Small's work over the years then you have probably become accustomed to the way she can connect with all learners—students and teachers alike. If this is the first time you are picking up a book from Marian Small, I am confident that you will not be disappointed. I truly look forward to your learning alongside Small as she sits at your shoulder to help guide you through the world of K–2 mathematics. Not only will she leave you with open-ended problems and tasks that you can immediately put to work, she will also uncover a new lens for how to approach mathematics and teach young children in your primary classroom.

At a time when finding the time to invest in ourselves is difficult, it is great to have this resource in our back pockets. If you teach math in any capacity, you are a math teacher, so on the behalf of your students, thanks for taking the time to improve and fine-tune your craft. Thanks for making learning fun!

—Graham Fletcher
Math Specialist
Atlanta, Georgia

Preface

THIS RESOURCE is intended to support kindergarten and primary grade teachers in delivering the Common Core curriculum (Common Core State Standards Initiative, 2010) by providing them with a deeper understanding of the fundamental ideas that underlie the mathematics that students are to learn. It will also help parents to better support their children and help preschool teachers to provide more valuable math learning experiences. Included as well are many fun, but mathematically rich, activities for preschool and kindergarten, for 1st grade, and for 2nd grade. There are additional suggestions for engaging and mathematically valuable home activities, along with recommendations for classroom and home read-aloud and other books that reinforce mathematical learning.

To put it all in perspective, the first chapter focuses on critical pedagogical principles in teaching mathematics to young children. This provides a framework for teachers to keep in mind about what is most important in teaching early mathematics. A tool is also provided for evaluating additional activities for how "worthwhile" they might be and offering guidelines for new activities that teachers may create. Subsequent chapters are organized around the headings of the Common Core curriculum standards (2010) for the primary grades, specifically Counting and Cardinality, Operations and Algebraic Thinking, Number and Operations in Base Ten, Measurement and Data, and Geometry.

Each of these chapters includes a discussion of the fundamentals—the underlying math, as well as expected student thinking and development in that area. In addition, a discussion of likely student misconceptions that need to be addressed is provided. Next comes the fun, in the form of engaging learning and practice activities that also serve as formative assessments to check on understanding of fundamentals. These activities are broken down by grade level—preK–K, 1st grade, and 2nd grade—as appropriate for each content area. Finally, suggestions for home activities are provided, as encouragement for parental involvement.

This book is not designed to be a full teaching resource with lessons for each day. Instead, the material provided offers playful, interesting, and meaningful activities to focus learning around. I sincerely hope those of you in the field who use this resource will find that it meets these goals.

Acknowledgments

I HAVE HAD many opportunities to develop mathematics teaching resources at all grade levels, but it has been a particular privilege to work on mathematics in the early years. I have not had that opportunity for quite a few years.

I appreciate the suggestion from Teachers College Press that we pursue this endeavor. Jean Ward and the rest of the team have continued to be so encouraging, kind, and helpful that I would like to publicly thank them, yet again.

❖ CHAPTER 1 ❖

Pedagogical Principles

Children Playing, Talking, Touching, and Thinking Their Way to Understanding

THE IDEAS in this resource are based on the premise that there are a number of established pedagogical principles that must be respected in developing mathematical learning opportunities for young children.

These include the following:

- the importance of worthwhile mathematical tasks,
- the value of rich mathematical conversation,
- the value of teaching through play,
- the value of learning with concrete objects,
- the importance of differentiation and appropriate challenge in the classroom, and
- the importance of listening to the child.

WHAT MAKES A TASK WORTHWHILE?

Different individuals will have different opinions about what makes a mathematical task worthwhile (Breyfogle & Williams, 2008). Many believe, though, that the following are critical components of a worthwhile task:

- The math being addressed should be "substantial"; usually the tasks involve reasoning and connections.
- The task should not be too easy or too hard, but should present an appropriate challenge for the student.
- The task should be engaging.
- The task should not be overscaffolded.
- The task has natural extensions.
- There are many ways to approach the task.

Some might suggest that the task be rooted in real-life situations (Wolf, 2015). I would argue that this depends on what is meant by "real-life situations." I believe it is as real-life for students to play with pattern blocks to make a design as it is to purchase an item in a pretend store.

Others might argue that the task should involve flexible use of technology (Learn Alberta, 2007). I feel that this can be useful but is not essential.

When a teacher chooses a task, she or he should ensure that the bulk of the time that students spend pursuing the task is spent thinking mathematically and not simply on "busy work" with a little bit of mathematical thinking thrown in.

Bay-Williams and Van de Walle (2010) presented a list of criteria for evaluating the worth of a task. They suggested that teachers rate a task on a scale of 1 to 4 based on attributes including whether the math covered is significant, whether is it appropriate for the child, how engaging the task is, and whether the task calls for true problem solving.

Below is an alternate scale you might consider in judging whether a task is worthwhile for young students.

Goal: The task . . .	Rating			
	1	2	3	4
is mathematically valuable.				
will extend students' mathematical knowledge.				
allows entry for all students.				
extends strong students.				
involves students in problem solving/critical thinking/ creative thinking.				
engages students.				
supports collaboration.				
provides opportunity for rich math conversation.				

For any teaching activity a teacher might consider, he or she might come up with a "worthwhile" score using the 1–4 rating scale, where 1 shows no evidence that the goal is likely to be met and 4 indicates that the goal is likely to be fully achieved with the task.

RICH MATHEMATICAL CONVERSATION

Most of us learn best when learning with others. Most of the tasks suggested in this resource are meant as learning opportunities rather than as assessment opportunities, so it makes sense that students engage in these activities in pairs or small groups. This also makes it more fun for the students.

Ideally, students working together are likely to engage in conversations that are less about one student telling another what to do and more about considering alternative approaches for making mathematical sense of the task. The focus is less on the answer and more on the mathematical thinking in which students engage (Hufferd-Ackles, Fuson, & Sherin, 2004).

As well, the conversation with the teacher needs to be rich, and more than just questions from teachers that only require short answers from students.

THE VALUE OF TEACHING THROUGH PLAY

Early childhood educators have long advocated play-based learning; the belief is that an inquiry stance is crucial to early literacy and numeracy development (National Council for Curriculum and Assessment [NCCA], 2009). This is based, in large part, on students' innate curiosity about their world.

Many opportunities for mathematics arise during play. For example, while building, parents or educators might raise issues of counting (how many blocks were used), stability (which sorts of blocks were on the bottom versus the top), measurement (how tall or wide the structure is), and so forth. While playing with a tea set, parents or educators might raise issues of measurement, for example, how much small cups hold versus larger cups, or how many cups a teapot could actually fill. While playing dress-up, parents or educators might raise issues of measurement, in terms of sizes of clothing items.

Mathematics standards for young children are more likely to be met when a teacher ensures that appropriate materials are available to stimulate the child mathematically and then follows up the students' conversation in play with appropriate questions and challenges.

For example, if a child is kicking a ball, a parent or educator might ask how we could measure how far it was kicked. If a child is flying a kite, parents or educators could ask how the child could figure out if it went higher the last time or this time. If a child is hanging onto a high bar on a playground, a parent or educator could ask how the child will know how long he or she has been holding on.

Many of the math games in this book are unnamed, but teachers might invite students to name some of the class favorites to make the games feel more like their own and to give them some ownership of mathematical ideas.

THE VALUE OF LEARNING USING CONCRETE OBJECTS

Mathematics is a very abstract subject. It is through looking at concepts concretely, with concrete materials, that students can make sense of mathematical concepts and move from the concrete to the abstract (National Research Council, 2001).

A combination of structured materials—such as counters or Cuisenaire rods—and more natural materials should be available. Some of the standard mathematical tools mentioned in the chapters that follow may not be available in all preschools. Items such as rekenreks; linking cubes; square tiles; Cuisenaire rods; commercial number paths; pan balances; base-ten flats, rods, and ones; and pattern blocks can be created as homemade versions. For example:

- In place of a rekenrek, a parent or educator can construct two lines of 10 beads, first 5 of one color and then 5 of another, and attach each line of beads to two small pieces of wood.
- Linking cubes can be replaced by blocks that do not link, if necessary.
- Square tiles can be cut out of plastic or paper and possibly laminated.
- Cuisenaire rods can be created by using colored strips of lengths 1, 2, 3, 4, 5, 6, 7, 8, 9, 10 (of any unit) and possibly laminating them to make reuse easier.
- Number paths can be created by painting numbers on small carpet squares and placing them in a line.
- Pan balances can be created by creating a "seesaw" with a small piece of board.
- Base-ten flats, rods, and ones can be created using plastic or paper that is laminated with small unit squares, strips as long as 10 squares, and flats as wide as 10 strips.
- Pattern blocks can be accessed virtually or traced from a virtual environment and made from plastic or paper, possibly laminated.

Many activities in subsequent chapters use everyday materials such as bingo chips, cards, dice, and so forth.

There will, of course, be times where no materials are used, for example, when practicing rote counting, but much of the meaningful math learning is enhanced with manipulative materials.

THE IMPORTANCE OF DIFFERENTIATION

Tasks are not appropriately challenging unless the teacher or parent takes into account the specific nature of the child who is learning. Whereas a particular task might be rich for one student, it might be out of the reach of another or simply not challenging enough for a third child.

It is the teacher's responsibility to be sufficiently aware of the differences among the students she or he teaches to ensure that tasks are either open-ended enough to suit most students or that tasks are appropriately adapted, as needed, for a particular child.

THE IMPORTANCE OF LISTENING TO THE CHILD

Because teachers are busy people, they are often in a hurry to get to where they are going instructionally. Sometimes teachers end up cutting a child's conversation short because it is getting lengthy. But we know that the best way to respond to a child and to help that child learn is to have a fulsome understanding of what he or she is thinking. This is only possible when listening to the child.

Although sometimes teachers listen in order to evaluate a student's knowledge, listening is critical in learning situations too, not just evaluation situations. Teachers and parents need to listen with no agenda, and their body language should make it clear to students that they really want to hear what the children have to say.

If students end up talking about peripheral issues, teachers can certainly try to redirect the conversation, but *after* listening first.

❖ CHAPTER 2 ❖

Counting and Cardinality

THIS CHAPTER focuses on the early experiences students should have as they learn to count a quantity to determine its numerical size, or **cardinality**.

THE FUNDAMENTALS

Rote Versus Meaningful Counting

There is a big difference between a child who is able to say the counting sequence 1, 2, 3, 4, 5, . . . and the child who can use that sequence to figure out how many objects are in a set. The former skill is called rote counting; the latter is more meaningful counting.

Students need to learn the rote sequence from 1 to 10 first, so they can apply that knowledge to determining the size of a set. Learning the rote sequence first also helps students count higher later and helps them to **skip count** by 2s, 5s, and 10s.

Counting Principles

To count correctly, students use each of the following counting principles (Gelman & Gallistel, 1978):

1. ***The One-to-One Principle.*** There is only one number said for each object in the set.
2. ***The Stable-Order Principle.*** There is a consistent set of counting words that never changes.
3. ***The Cardinal Principle.*** The last number that is said tells how many are in the set.
4. ***The Abstraction Principle.*** No matter what objects are counted, large or small, you say the same numbers and still attach one number to one object.
5. ***The Order-Irrelevance Principle.*** You can count in any order; the number in the set does not change.

Teachers need to observe each student as he or she counts to see which of these principles are in place for that child. For example, for Principle 1, a teacher observes whether students overlook objects, recount objects, or say more than one number when counting certain objects.

For Principle 2, a teacher observes whether the words students say are ALWAYS *one, two, three,* and so forth, in exactly that order.

For Principle 3, a teacher observes whether the child realizes that the size of the set is not 1, 2, 3, 4, 5, but just 5.

For Principle 4, a teacher observes whether students count different sizes or types of objects differently. That means that it is important that students have the opportunity to count sets with mixed-size and mixed-type objects.

For Principle 5, a teacher observes whether children realize that no matter where they begin or how they continue the count, the cardinality, or total number in the set, remains the same.

To reinforce the concept that we can count objects in any order, you might encourage students to respond to a question like this one:

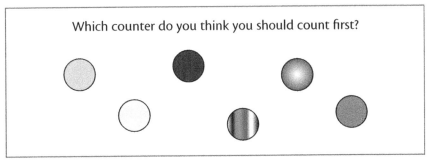

This task should alert students to the idea that different students might make different decisions, but they can all be right. It is more memorable to work through an activity like this—where students hear other students make different decisions than they would—than to simply be told it doesn't matter which counter to count first.

To reinforce the idea that size should not matter in a normal count (but might matter if it's possible to break objects into pieces), you might encourage students to respond to this question:

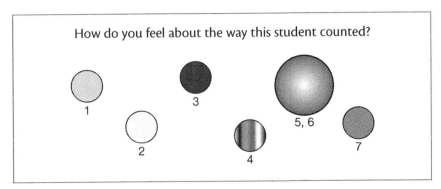

Notice that the question asked is not whether the student counted correctly; clearly, he or she did not. But there is some logic to why a student would say what he or she does, and the question allows for that discussion. For example, if these were cookies, it would be "fair" to break up the large cookie and serve two children, so two numbers might make sense to use; there is reason to this child's thinking, so it should not be immediately discounted. Later a teacher might say, *But if I asked you how many cookies there are, would the student still be right?*

To reinforce the correct sequence of counting words, deliberately mix up the counting words some time and have students catch your "error."

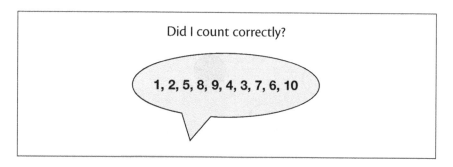

Counting books are often useful in developing both rote counting and meaningful counting since generally the numbers being counted are illustrated with the relevant quantities of objects.

Trajectories

It is helpful for a teacher to know the typical **trajectory** for counting that students pass through. This helps the teacher move students forward from where they are to where they could go.

Beware, though, that there are students who might not visibly go through each step in the exact order shown here.

Generally, students

- first learn the sequence of number words from 1 to 10 or so,
- then count small groups of objects meaningfully (perhaps up to 5),
- then display a given (small) number of objects when asked to,
- then extend the count to more objects (e.g., 10 or so),
- then learn to count backward in a rote fashion,
- then learn to count on (from a given amount other than one) for small amounts,
- then use the pattern of the number system to help them count further, and
- then learn to skip count using simple amounts, such as 2s, 5s, and 10s.

Often, especially with a lot of objects, students can count earlier when they are able touch the objects rather than when they can only look.

Clements and Sarama (2011) provide a more detailed trajectory that names the stages and includes even more details than listed here (e.g., precounters or children who say the numbers just out of order). This source may be a useful reference, with the caveat, again, that not all development for all children is linear.

Counting On

Counting on is a valuable prerequisite to addition. It is important for students to learn that to count on, for example, 3 numbers from 4, they do not include the 4 in the count. The same is true when counting backward.

Ensuring that **number lines** or **number paths** are highly visible in the classroom and used regularly will help students internalize the counting sequence.

Subitizing

Humans are able to recognize small quantities without counting them; we just recognize a configuration and associate it with a number. This is called **subitizing** (Mandler & Shebo, 1982). Most research (Starkey & Cooper, 1995) suggests that even very young children perceptually distinguish between 1, 2, 3, 4, or even a few more items, although subitizing—that is, recognizing configurations as attached to various numbers—occurs a bit later.

But where we can really help students is helping them to use number relationships to quickly subitize larger amounts, sometimes referred to as conceptual subitizing. For example, adults realize that the picture below shows 8 because they quickly see it as 4 and 4 more.

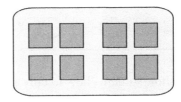

Students need many experiences recognizing different configurations for a variety of numbers, along with conversation about how they recognize the numbers. For example:

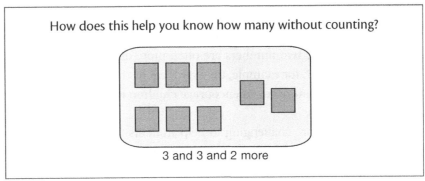

How does this help you know how many without counting?

3 and 3 and 2 more

(more examples appear on the next page)

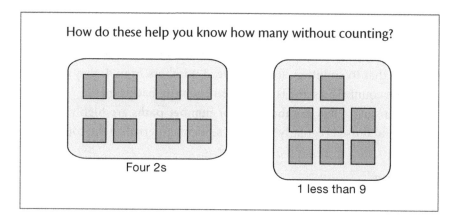

Playing games with dice, and using **ten-frames**, **rekenreks**, or **tally marks** regularly, are good ways for students to subitize numbers to 10 or even higher. Below are examples of 6 shown using each of these tools:

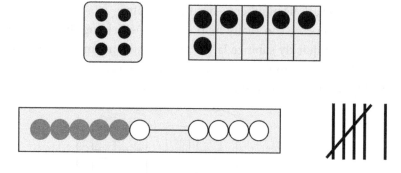

Educators can show students how to tally and create situations where students might tally, for example, how many students are wearing a particular color on a particular day. Parents or educators can ask children, after using dice or playing cards, to remember what the dots looked like when they saw, for example, 6.

Zero and One

Although it is important for students to realize that 0 and 1 are numbers just like 2 or 3 or 4, these two numbers are often more difficult for students to "see" than other numbers. If, for example, they see 1 circle, they tend to think "circle," not "1." A teacher or parent needs to encourage children to think about the quantity—1—in these situations.

It is even more challenging to help students to see 0. Perhaps the best way is to use pattern, and lead the students to see 0 as what happens as a quantity is repeatedly reduced by 1. This can be done with concrete objects, for example, as student volunteers put away blocks, or even shoes, in bozo buckets with numbers on them for each of the following:

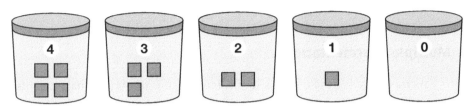

Teen Numbers

Counting past 10 to 20 is slightly more challenging for students than counting to 10, probably because they hear the count to 10 so much more often. The problems students have with this range are mostly about connecting the representations of what they hear to the numerals that are written, particularly those for 13 to 19. It is counterintuitive for students to hear *seventeen* (with the seven first) and then to see 17 (where the 7 is last). For many children, 17 should be said as *one seven* or maybe *ten seven*, but definitely not *seventeen*. This understanding is something that comes with a lot of attention and a lot of experience.

Counting Patterns to 100

Students become more effective counters when they hear the patterns in the counting system to 100. First they need to learn the words for the **multiples** of 10, that is, *twenty, thirty, forty, . . . , ninety, one hundred*. Then they need to realize that within those groupings (other than the teen grouping), we always hear that multiple-of-10 word followed by 1, 2, 3, . . . , and 9, and then we go to the next multiple-of-10 word. Often students need more time to get beyond 20 to 30 or 40; then at some point, when the pattern kicks in, several decades might be mastered simultaneously.

Sense of Quantity

Not only must students be able to say and record number names and count; they also need to have a sense of where they might encounter those quantities, and whether and when each quantity is a lot or a little. For example, they need to know that 3 can take up a lot of space (3 elephants) or not much space (3 small dots), and also that 3 children is a relatively small number of children for a class, but that a family with 3 children might be viewed as one with a lot of children. In fact, it is important for students to repeatedly consider situations in which numbers might be a lot or a little. They also need some sense, by looking at a group of objects, of whether the number of objects looks more like 3 or 5 or 10 or 20.

Multiple Representations

As mentioned in the discussion of subitizing, it is important that students see many representations of any number and learn to create a variety of representations. But what is even more important is that the teacher repeatedly question them as to what they see in the representations.

For example, consider these various representations for 12:

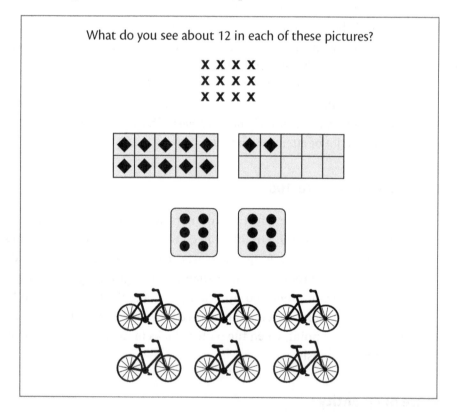

The array at the top helps the student see that 12 is made up of 4s. But the ten-frames help the student see that 12 is 10 and 2 more or a little more than 10 or 5 and 5 and 2. The dice help the student see that 12 is a double. The wheels on the bikes help the student to see that 12 is a set of pairs, which makes it an even number. Some children who think in terms of whole bikes might need to be directed to look at the wheels.

Repeatedly focusing on what each representation shows enriches the learning considerably.

Comparison

Students in these early years need to learn what we mean when we say that one number is more than another. Technically, one whole number is more than another if it comes later in the counting sequence; that's because, as we count, we say all the numbers until the last one. But it also means that if we lay out the quantities in **1-1 correspondence**, the quantity with "leftovers" is greater. Below, there are more dark stars than light ones, so that is why 7 is more than 5.

Students also need to learn whether they really need to match 1-1 to decide which quantity is more. If they can count, they never really have to do that, but even without counting, they probably only need to match if the quantities are close in size; otherwise, it might be obvious which quantity is more. For example, there are clearly more buttons in the right pile than in the left pile below. Educators or parents can build piles of buttons, chalk sticks, crayons, mittens, juice boxes, blocks, anything that is at hand, to ask the question over and over to reinforce the concept of more. Some students may still wish also to count the number in each pile.

Anchors to 5 and 10

It helps students to relate numbers from 1 to 12 or 13 to either 5 or 10 or both. They might think of 4 as 1 less than 5, of 7 as a bit closer to 5 than to 10, or of 12 as a little more than 10.

Using materials like ten-frames or rekenreks, both of which make it very easy to see 5 and 10, assists students in anchoring to 5 and 10.

To help students develop a solid understanding of 5 and 10, make sure to spend lots of time working on these numbers and, of course, relating them to fingers and toes.

You might introduce tallying as a way to emphasize 5. The tally below shows, for example, that 7 is just a little more than 5.

Numerals

Children encounter **numerals**, symbols for numbers, all around them, so it becomes important that they become familiar with various "versions" of numerals, whether on digital devices, in print, or handwritten; these different versions might look different. For example, compare these 8s:

Students also need to learn to write numerals, which requires practice. Teachers and parents need to remember, though, that there is not only one proper form for a numeral. What is important is that the numeral is easy to read and cannot be mistaken for another.

Number in Pattern

Although the Common Core curriculum (2010) does not specifically address pattern in the primary years, pattern has traditionally been an important part of the mathematics curriculum. There are number concepts and spatial concepts built into pattern work.

In this section about counting and cardinality, it might make sense for students to identify how many items form the **core** (the smallest repeating piece) of a pattern. In the pattern below, the core is 4 items long.

MISCONCEPTIONS TO WATCH FOR

> ➤ *Skipping Objects When Counting.* When students count, they often lose track and skip objects. It is useful to help them see that physically moving an object (such as a counter) once it has been counted makes it easier to keep track.

> ➤ *Counting Objects Twice.* Conversely, when students count, they may lose track and count an object more than once. Again, it is useful to help them see that physically moving an object once it has been counted makes it easier to keep track.

> ➤ *Conservation Issues.* There is research that shows us that some students believe that the count of a set of objects can change when some or all of the objects are moved; this is referred to as a lack of **conservation of number** (Piaget, 1965). It is important to provide opportunities for students to say what the count will be after some objects have been moved. Be aware that it is natural that students believe that if items are more spread out, there are more, since there is more length, even though the number is unchanged.
>
> Forcing a student to say that the value of a set after it has been spread out and the value of the original set are the same when he or she is not convinced is probably not helpful. We can just encourage students to count again until they have enough experience to convince them that the number does not change.

> ➤ *Comparison Issues.* Sometimes when students compare two sets of objects, and the objects are of different sizes, they are not careful about lining up the objects from the two sets in a one-to-one fashion. A teacher or parent needs to reposition the objects so they are lined up and ask if the student's answer has changed. If it has, the adult needs to plant a seed of doubt—*Should whether there are more of one kind or another depend on how I line them up?*

THE FUN

Pre-K and Kindergarten

These activities provide engaging learning and practice opportunities.

➤ Many students who can count on still choose to count by ones from the start just to be more secure that their answers are correct. To encourage students to count on, you might regularly hide a group of objects under some sort of cover, telling students how many are beneath, and then asking for a total. To make it more fun, you could use an opaque container instead of a paper and pretend that the counters inside the container are kids hiding in a building. Or have three real children sit under a table—with or without a cloth over it—and count on from there.

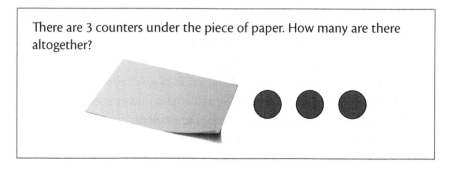

There are 3 counters under the piece of paper. How many are there altogether?

➤ To practice modeling quantities in multiple ways, ask students to choose a number to show in a lot of ways. What is most important is asking what each way shows. For example, you might ask:

Represent 7 lots of ways. Tell what each way shows about 7.

Students might show that 7 is 2 more than 5:

Or they might show that 7 is odd by showing pairs and 1 extra:

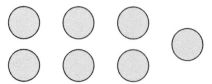

Or they might show that 7 is closer to 5 than to 10 like this:

➤ Line up too many or too few chairs for a group of students and ask:

Are there just enough chairs, too many, or too few?

You can ask many more comparison questions. For example:

Are there more of you wearing red or blue?
Do you think that more of you have buttons or zippers?
Do you think that more of you came to school on the bus or not?
Who linked together more cubes—Marcus or Tyler?
Who has more pencils—Annie or Alex?

➤ Students might explore the number of letters in their names.

Use linking cubes stuck together to show how many letters are in your first name.

Who has the most letters in the class?

How do the cubes show that?

They might show their names like this, using a **concrete graph** to see which is longest or shortest:

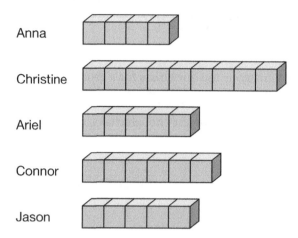

Anna

Christine

Ariel

Connor

Jason

Students should see that the longest link of cubes represents the name with the most letters, helping students see the point of graphs.

➤ Have students act out stories where some counters represent people near the swings and some represent people near the sandbox. Set up conditions like the ones below for students to act out. Each time, the children describe the number near the swings and the number near the sandbox. No doubt some students will make their stories complicated and put the swings near the sandbox so that sometimes the person near one is the same as the person near the other; that makes it fun.

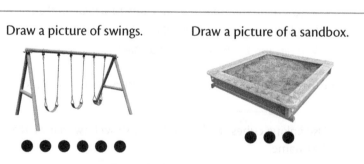

Draw a picture of swings.   Draw a picture of a sandbox.

Use counters as pretend people.

- Make sure that there are a LOT more people near the swings than near the sandbox.
- Now make sure there are ALMOST THE SAME number of people near both.
- Now change it so that there is just one more person near the swings than the sandbox.

Students might put 10 people near the swings and 2 near the sandbox for the first condition. They might use 4 and 6 for the second. They might use 4 and 3 for the third, but it could be any two consecutive numbers, with the greater one representing students near the swings. This activity can be repeated on the playground with real swings and students configuring and reconfiguring themselves to match your directions. This question provides lots of practice with comparison. By allowing students to create the numbers themselves, the thinking is stronger than if they simply compare given amounts.

➤ Students can practice representing quantities using tile designs.

> Choose a number.
>
> Make different-looking designs with that number of tiles.
>
> Tell how your designs are different.

Possible designs for 8 tiles might be these:

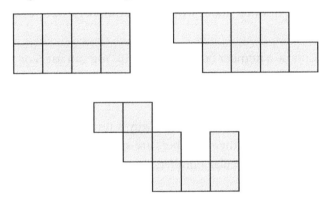

The purpose of this activity is for students to realize that there are many ways to show any particular amount.

➤ The teacher might prepare ten-frames cut into two pieces of different amounts. One ten-frame could yield pieces of 1 and 9, 2 and 8, 3 and 7, 4 and 6, or two 5s. What 1, 2, 3, 4, 5, 6, 7, 8, and 9 should look like is shown below and on the next page:

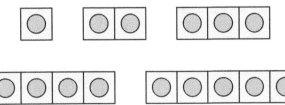

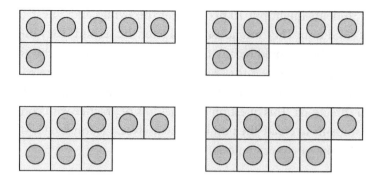

The pieces are placed in a bag and students draw them out in pairs until their two pieces total 10.

> Put together two pieces to make a full ten-frame.

This provides important practice in the combinations that make 10.

➤ Students might think about why various numbers are special.

> Choose a number between 5 and 10. You can use 5 or 10 if you wish.
> Tell why your number is special.

There is no right answer about why a number is special, but having the children talk about why their numbers are special will provide insight into what they know about the particular numbers they choose.

➤ Provide 10 bowling pins and a bowling ball for students. They can explore how many pins are left standing as a way to see arrangements for that number. This should support subitizing and should support an understanding that any amount can be represented in many ways. It's just more fun when it is bowling!

> Try to knock down lots of the 10 bowling pins.
> Look at how many pins are left.
> How are they arranged?

> Students can focus on a particular number.

It's a 4 day.

Dress somehow to show 4.

Bring lots of groups of 4 things to school.

This fun activity will provide students with practice with a particular number, in this case, 4. They will be excited choosing what to wear and what to bring. On a different occasion, you might have a 7 day or a 10 day, or practice any other number you might choose.

OR

Choose a number.

Use that number of blocks to build a block structure.

This activity supports children's natural desire to build block structures, but there is also attention to representing particular numbers. Students might explore whether structures with more blocks are always higher or not.

OR

Choose a number.

Make a bug with that number of legs.

As do the other activities, this activity appeals to students' sense of play but also gives them an opportunity to practice representing numbers. It might be interesting to see if students appeal to symmetry or whether any children end up with a bug that has an odd number of legs.

OR

Provide cut-out pictures of vegetables. Tell students they can use the cut-outs or can draw their own vegetables to create a garden:

> Choose 4 vegetables for your garden.
>
> Decide how many of each to plant.
>
> Draw what your garden would look like.

This activity, too, appeals to students' love to create, but encourages them to think of what they are creating in terms of quantity.

OR

Students might use specific numbers of **Cuisenaire rods** to create designs.

> Choose a number of Cuisenaire rods of different sizes.
>
> Use the rods to create a picture.

Again, this activity appeals to children's love to create, but it also familiarizes them with the rods, which are a very useful mathematical tool for operations.

➤ Students can model many numbers at the same time.

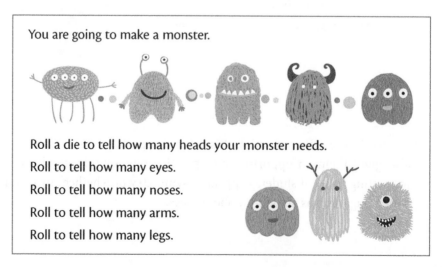

> You are going to make a monster.
>
> Roll a die to tell how many heads your monster needs.
> Roll to tell how many eyes.
> Roll to tell how many noses.
> Roll to tell how many arms.
> Roll to tell how many legs.

The monster game gives students the opportunity to work with many numbers at the same time. Rather than telling students how many eyes, arms, noses, and so forth, to use for their monsters, it is best to allow for some variety. Using the die to determine numbers of parts is a way let students avoid making a choice, but it still provides for unique monsters.

OR

Read the book *Ten Black Dots* (Crews, 1992) to students. This book is a classic, and students have loved it for many years (1992 was a new edition of an older version). Students can use *Ten Black Dots* as a model to create their own book.

> Write some pages for your own book called *Ten Red Squares.*

Writing their own book allows for creativity while providing number practice for students.

It might also be interesting to ask students how many dots are on the cover of *Ten Black Dots* and whether they think the dots should be organized the way they are (e.g., why there are 4 dots on the 1 and 6 dots on the 0).

OR

Students can create a pattern with a core of a particular number of items. If students have not met the term "core," simply replace that word with "the part of a pattern that repeats."

> Choose a number. Use that number of different shapes to make the core of a pattern. Show enough shapes that it is easy to see how many make the core.

A task like this one not only practices number but also helps create a deeper understanding of pattern. Although pattern topics do not appear in the early Common Core standards (2010), clearly pattern is a fundamental part of math and needs attention. This activity allows for that attention.

You might ask additional questions. For example: *Which shape is number 7 in your pattern? Which is number 10?* And so forth.

> Students can look for numerals around them.

Look for numerals in the classroom. Talk about what you find.

It is important for students to understand that numbers are part of the world in which we live. It motivates their interest in them and also helps them better understand their world. It may be that students see two-digit or three-digit numerals and treat them as single digits; for now, that is appropriate.

> Students can use counting to keep track of everyday activities, as suggested below. This is an easy and comfortable way for them to practice counting.

Count your steps as you walk up or down stairs or down the hall.

> Provide a riddle like the one below and challenge students to figure out how many red and blue counters there are if you tell them how many green ones there are. Then students might create riddles for each other, choosing which type of counter to tell about, and letting their friends figure out the other numbers.
> The value of a problem like the one below is that students begin focusing on number relationships, which underlies most work with math. You could tell them how many blues or reds there are instead of greens.

There is 1 MORE **red** counter than **blue** ones.

There are 2 FEWER **green** counters than **red** ones.

If there are 5 **greens**, how many **reds** and **blues** are there?

[*Possible solutions:* For 5 greens, there would be 7 reds and 6 blues.
For 8 reds, there would be 7 blues and 6 greens.
For 4 blues, there would be 5 reds and 3 greens.]

> Students can practice comparisons by setting up relative prices for items. You might choose to add conditions, for example, the most expensive must be a LOT more than the least expensive, or perhaps the prices must be fairly close. The prices can be in cents or in dollars.

> Choose 3 items from the room.
> Decide which should be the least, the middle, and the most expensive.
> Make up prices that make this work.

Many students enjoy "shopping" and this activity feeds that desire. It is valuable in that it allows students to think about why some things might be more expensive than other things, without forcing any "right" answers.

> Students can practice numeral writing in interesting ways. You might ask them to write the numerals in a sand table, as suggested below, but they might also shape numerals out of yarn or string or craft sticks and glue. It is important for students to have experiences using a variety of media to get comfortable writing numerals.

> Write numerals in sand at a sand table.

Suggestions for Home Activities: Pre-K and Kindergarten

You might encourage parents to come to school for a "fun math at home" program or create short videos for them and post them on your school website.

Help parents understand the difference between rote and meaningful counting. Help them, also, to realize that learning to count fluently, count backward, do skip counting, and so forth, takes time and they should expect and accept some "relapses."

> Encourage parents to sing number songs with their children, such as these:

Ten in the Bed
Five Little Monkeys
Four Hugs a Day
One Two, Buckle My Shoe
Five Green and Speckled Frogs

> Encourage parents to share counting books with children. Some good ones include the following:

> *1, 2, 3 to the Zoo* (Carle, 1996b)
> *Ten Black Dots* (Crews, 1992)
> *Mouse Count* (Walsh, 1991)
> *Richard Scarry's Best Counting Book Ever* (Scarry, 1968)
> *The Very Hungry Caterpillar* (Carle, 1994)
> *Ten Little Ladybugs* (Gerth, 2000)
> *Toasty Toes: Counting by Tens* (Dahl, 2006)

> Encourage parents to allow students to use high-quality math counting apps. In particular, they might want to use *Touchcounts* (Sinclair, 2014).

> Encourage parents to create numeral "jigsaw puzzles" for children to play with.

> Encourage parents to play board games with their children that require them to move based on the roll of a die.

> Have parents play "concentration" games where two like cards are matched using numerals and quantity amounts.

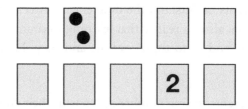

> Have parents regularly ask students to count out silverware or napkins. Have them deliberately give too many or too few items sometimes so children must figure out what to do.

➤ Have parents create dot-to-dot puzzles that create a design when students follow a path. For example, the puzzle could look like this:

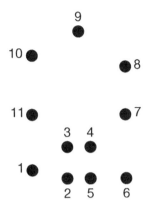

❖ CHAPTER 3 ❖

Operations and Algebraic Thinking

THIS CHAPTER focuses on what mathematical operations mean, how those meanings affect how we figure out sums and differences, and how we can make it engaging for young children to gain those understandings and connections.

THE FUNDAMENTALS

When to Use Addition

Although there are different kinds of situations that can be described by addition, the operation of addition involves parts that are put together to make a whole. It can be described that simply to students. For example, 3 + 5 involves putting together 3 with 5 and determining the total.

Sometimes the joining is "active": There are some items and some other items join them. For example, there could be 3 children in a room, 5 more enter (the action), and we wonder how many children are there now. In other cases, the relationship is more "static," where there are different parts that make up a whole. For example, there might be 3 boys and 5 girls on the playground and we wonder how many children there are.

Once students are ready, **bar diagrams** can be used to model the relationship of the parts to the whole.

Part	Part
Whole	

Another example of a joining situation might be: *There are 4 birds, and 2 more join them. How many are there now?* This would be represented on a bar diagram as shown below:

4	2
????	

A static situation might be: *There are 4 boys and 2 girls in the van. How many children are there?* On a bar diagram this would be:

In both instances, parts make up a whole. The visuals are identical.

Students generally are more comfortable working with active joining situations before they begin to deal with more static situations.

One more model for addition feels somewhat different. For example, sometimes we model 5 + 3 on a number path like this:

This time, it appears that the 5 is not really a quantity that is combined with 3. But, in fact, it is. Starting at 5 is equivalent to counting the 5 spaces that were taken to move from the start to 5; they are just not highlighted.

When to Use Subtraction

Subtraction is somewhat more complex than addition. Although it is always the opposite of addition—that is, you know a whole and some parts, but not all of them—we apply subtraction in what seems like a broader variety of situations.

> *Take-Away*

Sometimes subtraction describes separation or take-away: *There were 6 children. Then 2 went away. How many are still there?*

Using a bar diagram, you might see this:

Using a number path, you might see this:

The answer is the number on which you land after starting at 6 and going back 2.

➤ Missing Addend

Sometimes subtraction describes a **missing addend**: *There were 6 children. 2 are girls. How many are boys?*

Using a bar diagram, you might see this:

2	????
6	

Using a number path, you might see this:

The answer is not the number on which you land, since you know that will be 6. The answer is the number of steps it took to get from 2 to 6.

➤ Comparison

Sometimes subtraction describes a comparison: *There were 6 boys. There were 2 girls. How many more boys were there than girls?*

Using a bar diagram, you might describe the situation like this.

2	????
6	

You might use the same number path diagram as for missing addend (above) or you might show two number paths and see how much farther along the path 6 is than 2.

1	2	3	4	5	6	7	8
1	2	3	4	5	6	7	8

Notice that the same bar diagram describes all three situations. The separating (or take-away) situation is more "active," while the comparison situation is more "static." The missing addend situation could be active (e.g., *I have $2. How much more do I have to get to be able to buy a $6 item?*) or static (e.g., *There are 6 coins. 2 are nickels. How many are not nickels?*)

It is essential for students to have experiences with all of the meanings of subtraction. You might pose this task to see which meanings they think of:

> How might you model 5 – 2 on the number path?
>
> | 1 | 2 | 3 | 4 | 5 | 6 | 7 | 8 |
> |---|---|---|---|---|---|---|---|

Young students are encouraged to use concrete objects to model addition and subtraction. However, be cautious about telling students to always begin by showing the greatest value when they are subtracting. For example, to figure out 8 – 3, a student might show 8, and then proceed to remove 3. But she or he might start by showing 3 and then count on to decide how many to add to make 8. Or he or she might show both to see how much more 8 is than 3.

The Relationship Between Addition and Subtraction

It is clear to us as adults—as we see from the fact that the same sort of bar diagram describes addition and subtraction, and because one of the meanings of subtraction is "missing addend"—that addition and subtraction are completely intertwined. This can be described in several ways.

- Every subtraction can be solved by figuring out what to add to one part value to achieve the whole.
- A subtraction undoes an addition or vice versa. This means that if you subtract a number and then add it back, or add a number and then subtract it, it is as if nothing has happened.

> For example, $3 + 2 = 5$ and $5 - 2 = 3$.
> $5 - 2 = 3$ and $3 + 2 = 5$.

- Every situation that can be described using either addition or subtraction can also be described using the other operation.

> For example, if the story were: *There were 9 cookies. I ate 3. How many are left?*, the story could be described by $3 + \square = 9$ or by $\square = 9 - 3$.

Note that both addition and subtraction are built on **decomposition** (breaking up numbers) and **composition** (putting them together).

➤ Types of Addition and Subtraction Equations

There are essentially six different types of addition or subtraction **equations** involving two parts and a whole. Sometimes an addition equation can be solved by subtracting, and sometimes a subtraction equation can be solved by adding. It is important for students to see all of these structures.

Equation Type	Possible Problem Likely to Be Described by That Equation Type	How the Missing Value Is Determined
$a + b = \square$	There were 8 apples and 2 bananas. How many pieces of fruit were there?	Adding $a + b$
$a + \square = c$	There were 12 kids in the room. Some more came in. Now there are 15 kids. How many came in?	Subtracting a from c
$\square + b = c$	I had some money. My mom gave me $4 and now I have $10. How much did I start with?	Subtracting b from c
$a - b = \square$	There were 15 books. 12 were paperback. How many were not?	Subtracting b from a
$a - \square = c$	I had $10 and spent some on a book. Now I have $6 left. How much did the book cost?	Subtracting c from a

| $\square - b = c$ | My sister has \$3 more than I do. How much does she have if I have \$9? | Adding b to c. |

Generally speaking, students find a + b = $\square$ and a – b = $\square$ easiest to work out first; next they tend to be comfortable with equations of the forms a + $\square$ = c and a – $\square$ = c; only later do they become comfortable with equations of the forms $\square$ + b = c and $\square$ – b = c. Not knowing the start is difficult for many students.

➤ It is also important for students to learn that an equals sign is not about getting an answer, but about showing an "equivalence." For example, 3 + 7 = 10 since 3 + 7 is the same as 10. Similarly, 3 + 4 = 6 + 1 because 3 + 4 is another name for 6 + 1. This understanding is facilitated when teachers read equations to students to help them focus on the notion that the two sides of the equation describe the same amount.

For example, you could read:

$3 + 4 = \square$ as   *How much is there if you combine 3 with 4?*

$3 + \square = 7$ as   *What do you need to add to 3 to end up with 7?*

$\square + 4 = 7$ as   *What did you start with if when you got 4 more, you ended up with 7?*

$7 - 2 = \square$ as   *What is left if you remove 2 from 7?* **OR** *How much more is 7 than 2?* **OR** *How far apart are 7 and 2?*

$7 - \square = 2$ as   *What did I remove from 7 if there are only 2 left?* **OR** *What amount is 7 two more than?* **OR** *Where did I begin if it took me 2 steps to get to 7?*

$\square - 5 = 2$ as   *If I removed 5 and still have 2 left, what did I start with?* **OR** *What number is 2 more than 5?* **OR** *Where did I end up if I started at 5 and moved 2 spaces forward?*

➤ To see which meanings of subtraction students relate to an equation, you might use the activity below in early primary grades:

> Tell three different stories that go with the equation 8 – 3 = 5.

Or, in a later grade:

> Make up a problem involving sports where you would do a subtraction.
> Tell what the subtraction is and the answer.

> To check that students really understand what an equation means, you can use a task like the one below. Students might use 3 black and 4 white cubes on one side of the balance and 2 gray and 5 dotted cubes on the other; or they might use 6 black on one side and 4 gray and 2 dotted cubes on the other.

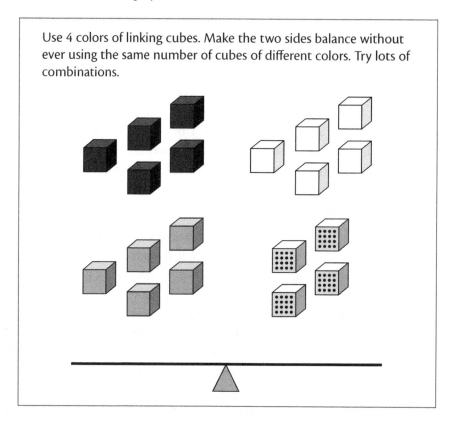

Use 4 colors of linking cubes. Make the two sides balance without ever using the same number of cubes of different colors. Try lots of combinations.

The notion of an equation as balance can relate both to a weight balance as shown above (where two sides of a scale are level) or to length (where two lengths are identical). In the situation below, students see $10 + 2$. They can experiment with other rods to see that $9 + 3 = 10 + 2$, as does $6 + 6$ or $3 + 3 + 6$, and so forth. Also, this question can be reused with a length other than 12.

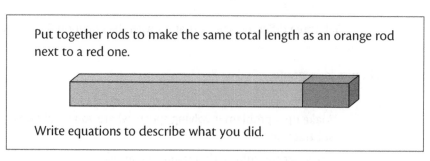

Put together rods to make the same total length as an orange rod next to a red one.

Write equations to describe what you did.

> Students need to explore whether equations are true or false using the notion of balance. The question below provides opportunity for this happening.

> Write some different equations with 2 numbers and an operation sign on each side. The equations must be TRUE.
>
> Now write some equations that are NOT true, but ALMOST true.
>
> Now write some equations where it's easy to tell right away that they are NOT true.

[*Possible solutions: For TRUE: 4 + 2 = 5 + 1.*
For ALMOST TRUE: 5 + 1 = 3 + 2.
For NOT TRUE: 10 + 3 = 1 + 2.]

It will be interesting to see what makes students feel that an equation is easily seen not to be true. For example, they might choose large numbers to add on one side and two small numbers that are close together on the other side.

Essential Properties of the Operations

> ### The Commutative Property for Addition

Students need to learn that numbers can be added in any order, but not subtracted in the reverse order. But we want them to know *why*. Just showing a few examples is not nearly as convincing as an argument like the one below.

> *Imagine you had some orange counters in one hand and some green in the other. Does the total number of counters you are holding change if you cross your hands?*

Another way to think of this is if counters were placed on two sides of a paper:

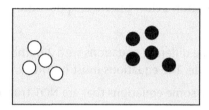

The paper is then turned around. Clearly, the number of counters did not change. None were removed or added.

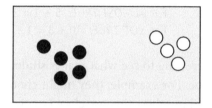

> *The Associative Property for Addition*

Sometimes we want to add more than two numbers. What the **associative property** tells us is that we have choices of how to combine three numbers into two numbers to add them. For example, we can think of 4 + 2 + 5 as 6 + 5 (adding the 4 and 2 first, and then adding the answer of 6 to 5) or as 4 + 7 (adding the 2 and 5 first, and then adding 4 to that 7).

Another way to think about this, though, is the following: If there are two piles of items, some items can be moved from one pile to the other without changing the total. That is why 4 + 7 (which is 4 + (2 + 5)) is the same as 6 + 5 (which is ((4 + 2) + 5); two are moved from the second pile to the first.

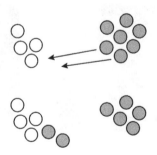

We want students to realize why the total cannot change by just moving counters from one pile to the other; we want students to understand that the effect is the same as increasing one part (**addend**) by the same amount by which the other part is reduced.

Yet one more way to think of the same idea is that you can add in stages. For example, to add 13 to 11, you can think of 11 as 10 and 1 more and first add the 10 part and then the 1 part. In other words, 13 + (10 + 1) = (13 + 10) + 1.

➤ Constant Difference

We want students to understand that the difference between any two numbers is the same as the difference between two numbers that are each the same amount greater than or the same amount less than the two original numbers. For example, 7 – 3 is the same as 10 – 6 (both numbers were increased by 3) or as 5 – 1 (both numbers were decreased by 2).

This makes sense if we look at the distances from 3 to 7 (which is 7 – 3), from 6 to 10 (which is 10 – 6), and from 1 to 5 (which is 5 – 1). The distances are the same; they are just shifted.

Another way to model the concept of **constant difference** is to use the notion of subtraction as comparison.

If you compare two linking cube trains, you can add the same number of cubes to both without changing the amount one train is more than the other. The picture below shows how much more 10 is than 7 (or 10 – 7). It is clear that 10 is 3 more than 7.

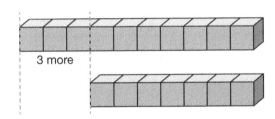

3 more

Notice that if the same number of cubes is added to the right of each train, the difference remains the same; in fact, by adding on the right, the exact same cubes (on the left) are the extras.

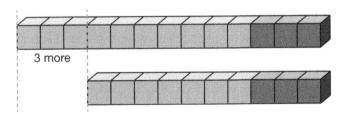

3 more

To reinforce the difference between what addition and subtraction mean, students in 2nd grade might consider whether there are more subtraction equations with a particular result than addition equations with that same result (when only whole numbers are involved) and why.

> Are there more answers to $\square$ + $\triangle$ = 10 or to $\square$ − $\triangle$ = 10?
> Why?

It turns out that there are MANY more subtractions. Any two numbers 10 apart, even really big numbers, satisfy the subtraction equation $\square$ − $\triangle$ = 10, but only smaller values can be combined to make 10. The reason there are so many subtractions is because of the constant difference idea.

➤ Adding or Subtracting 1

Students need to realize that adding 1 suggests there is 1 more counter, and so the result must be the next number you say when you count. Similarly, they need to realize that subtracting 1 results in the previous counting number.

➤ Adding or Subtracting 0

Students need to recognize why adding or subtracting 0 has no effect. They might think of adding 0 as jumping in place on a number path (as opposed to adding 1, where you move 1 step forward).

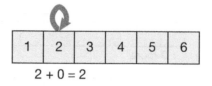

$$2 + 0 = 2$$

Maybe draw a hopscotch court either outside or in the classroom, with a box for 0, and have children jump as many times as they want on 0 and see that they still have not changed the number from 0, but as soon as they jump to 1, they have added.

➤ Adding Involving Equal Groups

To build a foundation for multiplication, students need experiences where they add equal groups, generally arranged in either arrays or pairs. For example, they might be asked to determine the totals in the two situations shown on the next page.

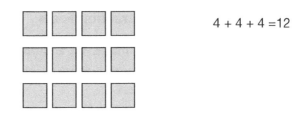

$4 + 4 + 4 = 12$

Six 2s make 12

Students should associate the term "even number" with a quantity that can be arranged in twos. This turns out to be the same as saying that the quantity can be arranged into two equal groups. For example, 12 is even both because it is 6 + 6 (two equal groups) or because it is made up of six 2s.

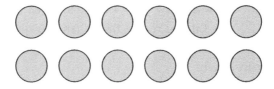

Developmental Stages for Addition and Subtraction

Most students are more successful at adding and subtracting with smaller numbers (e.g., up to 5 and then up to 10) before working with larger numbers.

Addition skills generally improve once students have become comfortable with counting on.

Addition and subtraction skills improve further once students are aware of and can use a variety of strategies based on the properties of the operations. At this point, they relate unknown sums and differences to known ones. How this is done is described in more detail on the next few pages.

Later, students use **place value** concepts to decompose and recompose whole numbers to be able to add or subtract multidigit numbers. Students develop strategies for working with fractions and decimals much later.

Learning the Addition and Subtraction Facts

It is vital that students eventually master the **addition and subtraction facts** to 20. Only when they know these facts can they either calculate with or estimate sums and differences with larger numbers.

There are many ways for students to learn the facts. The task is not only memorizing them; it is also recalling them from frequent use or from applying strategies based on the principles of addition and subtraction to relate unknown facts to known facts.

➤ Strategies Students Use to Learn Facts

There are many known strategies that students use to relate math facts. The first two strategies described below are direct applications of the properties of addition and subtraction discussed earlier. The next three are strategies students can readily learn and apply to extend their ability to work with novel situations.

Relate a Subtraction to a Known Addition. Since 4 + 3 = 7, we know that 3 + 4 = 7, that 7 – 4 = 3, and that 7 – 3 = 4.

The picture below shows 4 + 3 = 7 if you look left to right; 3 + 4 = 7 if you look right to left; 7 – 4 = 3 if you realize that when you remove the 4 part from the 7, the 3 part is left; and 7 – 3 = 4 if you realize that when you remove the 3 part from the 7, the 4 part is left.

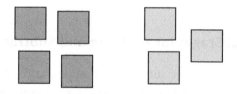

This relationship can also be seen with a bar diagram:

3	4
7	

Adding or Subtracting 1 or 2. Adding 1 or 2 or subtracting 1 or 2 can be accomplished easily by counting on or counting back.

Students realize that 4 + 2 = 6 since they can count 4, 5, 6 (2 numbers past 4).

Similarly, they realize that 7 – 1 = 6 since they can count 1 number back from 7: that is, 7, 6.

Looking at a number line or number path might help support such counting on or counting back.

1	2	3	4	5	6	7	8

Using Doubles. Students seem to remember doubles (1 + 1, 2 + 2, . . . , 9 + 9) more easily than a number of other facts. So they can relate "near doubles" to doubles to figure out certain unknown facts. For example, students might think of 4 + 3 as 1 more than 3 + 3 (since they know 3 + 3 = 6) or 1 less than 4 + 4.

Making Tens. Once students are facile with the combinations that make 10—that is, 9 + 1, 8 + 2, 7 + 3, 6 + 4, and 5 + 5—they can relate other facts to these. For example, 9 + 5 = 9 + 1 and 4 more, or 14. Similarly, 7 + 8 = 7 + 3 and 5 more, or 15. This kind of reasoning implicitly makes use of the associative property of addition discussed earlier: for example, 7 + 8 = 7 + (3 + 5) = (7 + 3) + 5.

A valuable tool for modeling this strategy is the ten-frame. For example, to show 9 + 5, a student might transform this view of 9 + 5:

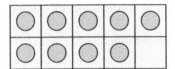 

to this view, which involves making a ten.

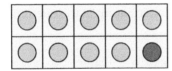 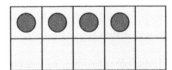

Compensation. Sometimes we add or subtract a more convenient number and then compensate for using an alternate value by taking another action.

For example, to solve 5 + 6, a student might add 5 + 5 and then compensate by adding another 1 since she or he added 5 rather than 6.

To solve 11 – 5, a student might subtract 10 – 5 and then compensate by adding the extra 1 from 11 that he or she did not use originally.

To solve 12 – 4, a student might subtract 12 – 2 and then compensate by subtracting the remaining 2 from 4 that she or he did not originally subtract.

> *Applying the Strategies*

To get a sense of which strategies students have internalized, you might ask a question like this:

> What is a useful strategy for figuring out 15 − 8 in case you forget the answer?

For the question above, for example, a student might use doubles and calculate 16 − 8 and then subtract another 1. Or a student might add up from 8 to 10 and then add 5 more. This question can be reused in many ways, just by changing the numerical values you choose.

> Students might also discuss strategies in situations like the two described below. This involves a level of metacognition whereby students think about what it is about a pair of numbers that encourages them to use a particular strategy.

> Think about what strategy you would use to figure out 9 + 6.
>
> What is another calculation you would do using the same strategy?

[*Possible solutions:* 9 + 8 or 9 + 5 or 8 + 6.]

OR

> For what question might you increase both numbers by the same amount to not change the result but make the question easier to answer?

[*Possible solution:* 16 − 9 changing to 17 − 10.]

> There are a variety of possible strategies from which students might choose for working with greater numbers. For example, you might ask the following:

> What tools and strategies might you use to
>
>   subtract 49 from 66?   add 46 to 45?

To determine the difference between 49 and 66, students might:

- Subtract 46 from 66 and then subtract 3 more.
- Subtract 50 from 66 and then add 1 back.
- Add up 1 and then 16 more to get from 49 to 66.

OR

> How would you break up the number 28 to make it easy to
>
> subtract from 75?   add to 38?

Students might:

- Subtract 25 from 75 and then 3 more, or subtract 30 and add 2.
- Add 30 to 38 and then subtract 2, or add 2 and then 26.

➤ *The Value of Patterns*

Studying the addition table should help students see patterns that might make it easier for them to relate unknown facts to known facts. For example, studying the highlighted diagonal helps students see that while 5 + 4 = 9, so do 6 + 3, 7 + 2, and so forth.

+	0	1	2	3	4	5	6	7	8	9
0	0	1	2	3	4	5	6	7	8	9
1	1	2	3	4	5	6	7	8	9	10
2	2	3	4	5	6	7	8	9	10	11
3	3	4	5	6	7	8	9	10	11	12
4	4	5	6	7	8	9	10	11	12	13
5	5	6	7	8	9	10	11	12	13	14
6	6	7	8	9	10	11	12	13	14	15
7	7	8	9	10	11	12	13	14	15	16
8	8	9	10	11	12	13	14	15	16	17
9	9	10	11	12	13	14	15	16	17	18

Students might also observe how the main diagonal starting from 0 + 0 and going to 9 + 9 is made up of the even numbers (or the doubles of the numbers being added).

Other patterns involve comparing one row with the row above (the values are always 1 more in the lower row) or one column with the column to the left (the values are always 1 more in the column to the right), and so forth.

> ## The Need for Practice

It is important that students practice facts, but ideally not in timed tests. Evidence suggests that such testing is counterproductive for many students (Boaler, 2014). Instead, students can practice through regular use of facts when playing games, when exploring patterns, and when solving problems.

Examples of Games.

20 First

Two players play. Each player, on his or her turn, rolls a die.

Each player keeps a running total.

The first player to get to 20 wins a point.

The winner of 5 points wins the game.

I Love 3

Two players play. Each player, on his or her turn, rolls a pair of dice.

If the player gets a pair with a difference of 3, the player rolls another die and adds it to 3 to get his or her points.

If the pair does not have a difference of 3, the turn is over.

Each player keeps a running total.

The first player to get a total of 20 wins the game.

Examples of Pattern Exploration. Students explore and extend patterns like these:

$$9 + 8 = \square \qquad \textbf{OR} \qquad 12 - 2 = \square$$
$$8 + 8 = \square \qquad\qquad\qquad 12 - 4 = \square$$
$$7 + 8 = \square \qquad\qquad\qquad 12 - 6 = \square$$

They observe that when one addend is reduced by 1, so is the sum, or that when 2 more are subtracted, the result is 2 less.

Examples of Problems That Use Facts. The numbers 0 to 9 are written on popsicle sticks. Students practice facts in solving this problem:

Chose two sticks without looking.

Choose one of these problems:

    Is the sum more likely to be less than 8 or more than 8?

    Is the difference more likely to be more than 2 or less than 2?

MISCONCEPTIONS TO WATCH FOR

➤ *Adding by Counting On Incorrectly.* Sometimes students will say, for example, that 5 + 3 = 7 since they say 5, 6, 7 (three numbers), rather than a whispered 5, followed by 6, 7, 8.

➤ *Misinterpreting the Equal Sign.* Some students will solve 4 + ☐ = 8 by adding 4 and 8 since they see a 4, an 8, and a +. Students need you to talk through what the equation says.

➤ *Compensation Errors.* When using strategies, students sometimes compensate incorrectly. For example, when subtracting 4 from 10, a student may subtract 5 from 10 first and then, instead of adding 1 back, subtracts another 1.

THE FUN

Pre-K and Kindergarten

These activities provide engaging learning and practice opportunities.

➤ Students might build towers, always a popular choice, but at the same time, they practice subtraction by figuring out how many more to add to their chosen numbers to get to a total of 10 blocks.

The activity can be rejigged on other occasions to start with different numbers and arrive at different totals, for example, 8 or 9. You can also enrich the task by asking students how many more of one type of block there are than another.

> Choose fewer than 5 blocks and start a tower.
>
> Now add more blocks so that you use
> 10 blocks altogether.

➤ Students might combine math with music. The activity shown on the next page encourages students to think through the lyrics of songs they know. It brings in math by asking them to count the words in the lines of the songs to see if they can find two lines where the total number of words is 9 words. For example, if the first song they thought of was *Mary Had a Little Lamb,* they would count the words in each line of the song until they found, if they could, two lines that had a total of 9 words.

Choose two lines in a song you like and tell how many words you would say when you sing those two lines.

What song might have two lines where the total number of words is 9 words?

[*Possible solution:* Lines from *The Itsy Bitsy Spider*: Down came the rain, and washed the spider out.]

> Students need opportunities to decompose an amount into smaller amounts. In the activity below, they decompose the number 7 into two parts. You might note whether students are willing to allow for one set size to be 0 or not. Some children would argue that since it says that there are some bear counters and some dinosaur counters, neither amount can be 0. Others will allow for this option. You might extend the problem by using different numbers of counters on different occasions and/or allowing for more than two types of counters.

You have some bear counters and some dinosaur counters.

Altogether, you have 7 counters.

How many of each might you have?

OR

The activity at the top of the next page also involves decomposition, but sorting is addressed, as is algebra in equation writing. Students are encouraged to choose their own numbers, so that as students share, more combinations come up.

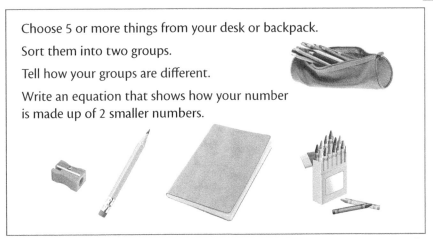

Choose 5 or more things from your desk or backpack.

Sort them into two groups.

Tell how your groups are different.

Write an equation that shows how your number
is made up of 2 smaller numbers.

[*Possible solution:* 3 things you can write with and 2 you cannot: 3 + 2 = 5.]

OR

The activity below encourages decomposition into three addends, rather than two,
to extend students. It might be valuable to have them note that when there are
three smaller trains rather than two, the train sizes tend to be smaller, although
not all of them have to be.

Build a "train" with linking cubes.

You can make it any length that is at least 5 cubes.

Tell how many cubes there are.

Show different ways to break it up into three smaller trains.

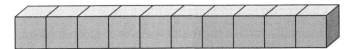

Write equations to describe what you did.

[*Possible solution:* 8 = 3 + 3 + 2.]

➤ You might encourage students to show their understanding of what addition and
subtraction mean by allowing them to act out stories. You will have an opportunity
to see what meanings of subtraction they seem to attend to, whether take-away,
missing addend, comparison, or all three. For addition, you can note whether students gravitate toward active or static situations.

Use two puppets to act out stories involving addition and subtraction that are about ducks in a pond. You can use pictures of ducks or pretend that counters are ducks.

OR

The activity below is attractive to students not only because it involves toys, but because they get to make decisions about the prices. Addition is involved as they determine the cost for two toys. Subtraction is involved as they compare prices.

Choose prices for these toys. Each price should be less than 5 dollars.

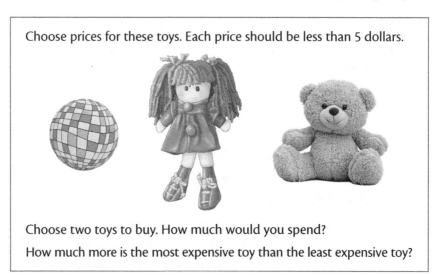

Choose two toys to buy. How much would you spend?

How much more is the most expensive toy than the least expensive toy?

OR

The activity at the top of the next page allows students to create designs, which most students enjoy doing.

They use both addition to create shapes worth more and subtraction to create shapes worth less and to ensure that two shapes are worth 6 together. This also provides practice in decomposing the quantity 6.

Choose a value for each shape. You must make sure that:

One shape is worth 2 more than another one.

One shape is worth 3 less than another one.

There are two shapes that are worth 6 together.

Create a design with your shapes.

[*Possible solutions:* 4, 6, 3, and 2; 3, 3, 5, and 6.]

OR

Students also need practice in finding combinations that add to 10. The activity below employs the missing addend meaning of subtraction, but there is an element of chance based on the use of the die. This makes the activity more exciting for students. It also makes it reusable.

You want to save 10 dollars to buy a gift for your mom.

Roll a die to decide how many dollars you start with.

Then tell how much more you would need to have 10 dollars.

OR

The activity below is personal, allowing students to think about their own phone numbers, as well as ones required to meet the conditions. Students also get excited about something being "special," so calling this phone number special just adds to the interest level for children.

My phone number is special.

It is ☐☐☐ ☐☐☐-☐☐☐☐.

If you add the first two numbers, the total is 10.

If you add the last two numbers, the total is 10.

What could my number be?

[*Possible solution:* 640 361-5746.]

Suggestions for Home Activities: Pre-K and Kindergarten

Make sure parents understand some of the critical underlying pieces of the math their children are learning. In particular, ensure that parents realize that they should *not* suggest that subtraction is only about take-away, but is also about missing addend and comparison.

> Encourage parents not to push for fact mastery at this young age. At the same time, parents might be encouraged to ask questions, with concrete objects available, that involve addition and subtraction. For example, they might ask the child, when two pairs of boots are at the door, how many boots will be there once everyone is home. Or they might ask the child how many plates there are when 3 small ones and 2 big ones are in view.

> Encourage parents to play number games with their children. You might make some up and send them home in plastic bags, or you might describe them and have the parents create their own versions. You might also encourage parents to create their own variations of games.

Some sample games:

Making Ten

Two players play using a deck of cards made up of four copies each of the numbers 1 to 9.

Each player gets four cards.

On your turn, you draw a card.

Whenever two cards add to 10, you can put them out.

After putting out your pairs, you can get rid of a card of your choice.

The first person who gets rid of all of his or her cards wins the game.

More Than Seven

Two players play.

Taking turns, each player rolls two dice.

If the sum is more than 7, the player get a point.

The first person with 5 points wins the game.

Big Differences

Two players play using a deck of cards made up of 4 copies each of the numbers 1 to 10.

On a turn, a player draws 2 cards.

If the difference between the 2 values of the cards chosen is more than 3, the player gets a point.

The first person with 10 points wins the game.

1st Grade

These activities provide engaging learning and practice opportunities.

➤ The bakery is just one context where students can show their understanding of what subtraction means. The context can easily be changed to another one. The numbers involved and the operation also can be changed so that the question can be reused many times.

Describe when you might subtract 9 from 12 in a bakery.

What addition also describes that situation?

➤ It is fun for children to use a song like *The Wheels on a Bus* to have a running story, where people get on and off the bus. Students can calculate the number on the bus after various numbers of people get on or off. For example, the story might start with: *Nobody was on the bus. The driver got in. How many are on the bus now? He picked up 3 passengers. Now how many are on the bus? At the next stop, he picked up 2 more passengers, but 1 got off. How many now?*

Students might then tell their own stories, describing how many are on the bus after each event.

Tell a story with many parts about people getting on and off the bus.

Tell how many people are on the bus each time.

OR

A problem like the one below can be used to encourage creativity. It forces students to think about math in context but provides a lot of freedom in which to work. Many more such examples can be created by changing the numbers and words, but probably continuing to use words involved with addition and subtraction, such as *more, fewer, altogether, more than,* and so forth.

> Make up a problem to solve that includes these words and numbers.
>
>   13   cookies   more   6
>
> Solve your problem.

[*Possible solution:* Jane had 13 cookies. She got 6 more and then 4 more. How many does she have now? Answer: 23 cookies.]

> Students can use designs, rather than stories, to practice their thinking about what addition and subtraction mean. They are likely to use a static meaning for addition. To show subtraction, they might use missing addend or comparison, or possibly take-away.

> Use square tiles to make a design that shows 7 + 4.
>
> Tell how you would change the design to show 7 − 4.

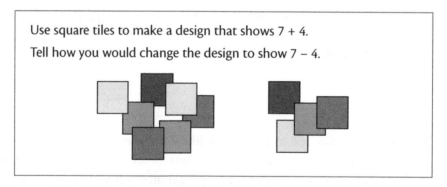

> There are lots of good activities about addition and subtraction that involve movement.

The problem shown on the next page requires students to think about how adding moves you forward and subtraction takes you back when dealing with whole numbers. Students also use comparison, realizing that they must move 2 MORE steps backward than forward to get from 4 to 2. There are an infinite number of answers, for example, 3 forward and 5 back, 13 forward and 15 back, and so forth.

You stand on the number 4 on a number path.

You move SOME steps forward.

You move SOME steps backward.

You end up at 2.

How many steps forward and backward might you have taken?

| 1 | 2 | 3 | 4 | 5 | 6 | 7 | 8 | 9 | 10 |

[*Solution:* Any number of steps forward and 2 more steps backward.]

OR

The activity below allows for physical action, which students generally appreciate. At the same time, they have opportunities to both add and subtract.

Decide how many times you will jump and how many times you will hop.

Altogether, how many moves will you make?

How many more hops than jumps or jumps than hops will you make?

Now do it.

> Students engage in problem solving when they think about how to decompose 20 to meet various conditions. Three conditions (these are three separate tasks) are suggested here, but many others are possible (e.g., one pile has 3 more counters than another, two piles are the same size, etc.).

Use 20 counters.

Arrange them into 3 piles so that:

The piles are close to the same size.

OR   One pile is double the size of another.

OR   One pile is really big.

> When students decompose numbers, they can break up the numbers into any pieces they wish. But sometimes there are restrictions on the type of decomposition that can be done. For example, when we use coins, we can only decompose into 1s, 5s, 10s, and 25s. When we use base-ten blocks, we can only decompose

into 10s and 1s. The activity below suggests a special decomposition, where we can only decompose into 3s and 7s. Students get to practice addition in a problem situation.

Asking for numbers that *cannot* be shown is an interesting and valuable additional feature. Students should realize that they cannot show 1, 2, 4, 5, 8, 11, and so forth. There are more numbers they can show than they cannot. In fact, every number past 11 can be shown.

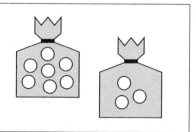

You have LOTS of bags of 3 counters.

You have LOTS of bags of 7 counters.

The bags cannot be opened.

What numbers can you show?

What numbers can you NOT show?

[*Solution:* You can show 3, 6, 7, 9, 10, 12, 13, 14, and all greater numbers (simply add a bag of 3 to 12, 13, 14 to get 15, 16, 17; add a bag of 3 to 15, 16, 17 to get 18, 19, 20, etc.). You cannot show 1, 2, 4, 5, 8, and 11.]

OR

The problem below provides an opportunity for students to decompose the number 20, but only into 2s and 4s.

You were looking at some people and some dogs.

You saw a total of 20 legs.

How many people might there have been? How many dogs?

[*Possible solutions:* 4 people and 3 dogs, or 2 people and 4 dogs.]

➤ The somewhat more challenging decomposition problem on the next page allows students to make judgments to estimate the relative sizes of jumps.

Although students are not required to notice that the first two jumps are the same size and the last one is about half that size, it would be important to observe whether they do notice this. It is acceptable for students to choose any three numbers for the jumps, although ideally the last jump size is smaller than the others.

You might also alter the problem in one of the following ways:

• Changing one or more of the jump sizes.
• Asking students to determine what jump sizes might be used to end, ultimately, at a particular number, such as 20.
• Asking some students to use "greater" numbers, if they are ready.

What do you think the value for the question mark might be? Why?

0   ?

[*Possible solutions:* 10 from 4 + 4 + 2, or 25 from 10 + 10 + 5.]

> The problem below is simply an engaging way for students to look for decompositions of 12. You could easily use the same format to create other puzzles.

Find different paths from the top to the bottom so that the numbers add to 12.

6	2	5
5	3	1
5	3	4

[*Possible solutions:* 6 to 3 to 3; 2 to 5 to 5; 5 to 1 to 3 (on same line) to 3.]

OR

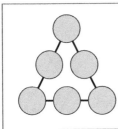

Place numbers in the circles so that each side adds to 12.

Try to make the sides' numbers different.

[*Possible solution:* First line: 5, second line: 3, 5; third line: 4, 6, 2.]

> The question below provides an opportunity for students to practice adding and subtracting numbers. By giving them a choice about where the 4 is placed, students have many options. Even once the 4 has been placed, there are lots of options. The question can be reused with numbers other than 4.

Use either the equation $\triangledown + \triangle = \square$ or the equation $\triangledown - \triangle = \square$.

Put the number 4 in one of the missing spots and give lots of possible values for the other missing values.

[*Possible solutions:* 4 + 7 = 11, or 5 + 4 = 9, or 1 + 3 = 4 **OR**
                        7 − 4 = 3, or 4 − 2 = 2, or 9 − 5 = 4.]

➤ Another situation for practicing addition and subtraction is shown here. Once again, the students have many options for placing their numbers. And by varying the requirements (number apart and number to add to), the task can be reused.

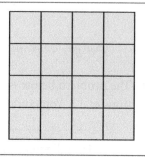

Place numbers in this grid so that there are lots of numbers near each other that are 2 apart and lots of numbers near each other that add to 10.

[*Possible solution:* First line: 3, 7, 8, 6; second line: 5, 3, 2, 6; third line: 5, 1, 4, 4; fourth line: 5, 9, 2, 4.]

➤ The problem below provides practice in composing numbers. By asking students to drop the counters on a design like this placed on the floor, the game becomes more fun. Allowing students to choose their own numbers for the target sections instantly allows for differentiation.

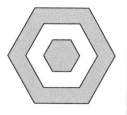

Choose numbers to put in each section of this design.

Make a big version and put it on the floor.

Drop 2 different counters on the design.

Add what you land on to get your score.

Play with a partner until someone gets 50 points.

Suggestions for Home Activities: 1st Grade

You might encourage parents to come to school for a "fun math at home" program or create short videos for them and post them on your school website. You might also create a blog with short postings or videos where you model or talk about some of the math activities in which their children are engaging.

➤ Suggest to parents that they read children's books that support addition and subtraction. These are some examples:

Ten for Dinner (Bogart, 1989)   *Monster Musical Chair* (Murphy, 2000)
Domino Addition (Long, 1996)   *Twenty Is Too Many* (Duke, 2000)
                  One Guinea Pig Is Not Enough (Duke, 2001)

> Parents might play games with their children that support addition and subtraction. They might use dominoes and have children tell the total on a domino or the difference between two amounts. They might also play card games like War, where the child is asked how much more one number is than another.

You can also suggest that parents create their own games. For example:

Four in a Row

4	3	5	0	4	1
2	2	6	1	3	4
5	3	1	3	0	5
1	0	2	2	5	1
2	3	0	2	6	2
3	5	1	4	0	3

Roll a die.

Choose 2 numbers on the board that add to the value on the die.

Cover those 2 numbers with counters.

The first person who covers 4 in a row wins the game.

Each player has two charts:

Chart 1

5	6	7	8	9	10	11	12	13	14

Chart 2

0	1	2	3	4	5

Roll 3 dice.

Add the values.

Use a blue counter to cover the sum on Chart 1.

Pick 2 of the numbers you rolled and subtract.

Use a counter to cover the difference on Chart 2.

The first person to cover all of his or her numbers wins the game.

2nd Grade

These activities provide engaging learning and practice opportunities.

➤ There are engaging ways for students to practice computation. Playing physical games is always attractive to children. The chart below can easily be adapted by using other numbers.

Throw 2 beanbags onto a big mat that looks like this.			

Throw 2 beanbags onto a big mat that looks like this.

Your partner does the same.

Whoever has a greater total wins points.

The number of points is the difference between the 2 numbers you landed on.

You win the game with 100 points.

33	15	9	14
12	46	51	36
12	18	41	37
28	7	38	51

➤ The opportunity to practice might be more contextual for students who are more attracted to "real-life" math.

Choose a number of books you might have.

Divide up your books into categories and tell how many might be in each category.

OR

Make up a menu with at least 10 items on it.

Give each item a price that is less than 50 cents.

Decide on 3 or 4 items you would order and tell how much you would have to pay.

> Students can also engage in problems that require reasoning. There are several examples here.

> Figure out what two numbers you might add so that:
>
> > The answer when you subtract is 10 less than the answer when you add.

[*Possible solution:* 30 and 5, 9 and 5, or 18 and 5.]

The solutions can be explained when students realize that if you add 5 to a number and subtract 5 from that same number, the answers must be 10 apart. Therefore, any number with 5 could work.

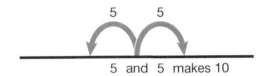

5 and 5 makes 10

OR

The problem below encourages students to decompose 47 into 4s and 5s in different ways.

> Some parents can take 4 students in their cars.
>
> Some can take 5 students.
>
> What are some different ways you could get all 47 students in Grade 2 to an event using parents' cars, with no empty seats?

[*Possible solutions:* 7 cars with 5 students and 3 cars with 4 students, or 3 cars with 5 students and 8 cars with 4 students.]

OR

The problem below encourages students to think about how to decompose 100 into numbers that meet a particular condition: in this case that they are close in size. Hopefully, students will realize that the two values need to be near 50 to make this happen.

> I added two numbers and the answer was 100. The numbers were not that far apart.
>
> What might they have been?

[*Possible solution:* 45 and 55.]

➤ It is helpful for students to represent operations visually. Students might think of the following picture as either adding 22 to an amount to achieve a given whole (subtraction) or as determining a whole of which 22 is a part.

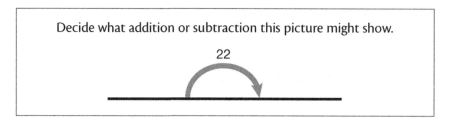

Decide what addition or subtraction this picture might show.

22

➤ Students might explore the connection between number and shape, measurement, or pattern.

The first problem below has students realize that the numbers being added to make a long thin rectangle are two equal larger numbers and two equal smaller ones.

Use toothpicks to make the top and right side of a VERY long rectangle.

Tell how many toothpicks you would need to go around the whole rectangle.

[*Possible solution:* 20 toothpicks across and 1 on the sides—a total of 42 toothpicks.]

OR

The problem below relates pattern to number. The richness of this problem is that students must realize that counting back by 6s from 43 (or subtracting 6s repeatedly from 43) is all they need to do.

A pattern is created by starting with a number and adding 6 over and over.

If 43 is in the pattern, but not too close to the start, what might the first 10 numbers in the pattern be?

[*Possible solution:* 1, 7, 13, 19, 25, 31, 37, 43, 49, 55, ...]

➤ Students might participate in activities where they work with random numbers, as happens when numbers are determined by the roll of dice. But such activities can still be connected to strategies. In the problem below, students might notice how counting the number of rows apart on a **100-chart** often describes the tens digit. For example, the difference between 34 and 56 is around 2 tens because 34 and 56 are 2 rows apart.

0	1	2	3	4	5	6	7	8	9
10	11	12	13	14	15	16	17	18	19
20	21	22	23	24	25	26	27	28	29
30	31	32	33	34	35	36	37	38	39
40	41	42	43	44	45	46	47	48	49
50	51	52	53	54	55	56	57	58	59
60	61	62	63	64	65	66	67	68	69
70	71	72	73	74	75	76	77	78	79
80	81	82	83	84	85	86	87	88	89
90	91	92	93	94	95	96	97	98	99

Roll two dice to get a 2-digit number.

Do it again.

Tell how much more one is than the other.

Tell how you could use a 100-chart to help you figure that out.

➤ The activity below is attractive because students always enjoy making designs. By allowing them to choose the values each **pattern block** shape is worth, students can choose numbers most appropriate for them to add.

Decide on a value for each of the hexagon, triangle, trapezoid, and rhombus pattern blocks.

Make a design and figure out its value.

➤ When using bar diagrams, young students are not precise about the relative sizes of the bars, and we should not expect them to be. But as they get older, their decisions about how big parts and the whole should be, relative to each other, get better. We can take advantage of that, as we do in the situation shown below.

For example, if a student puts 23 in the top left section of the bar diagram, she or he is likely to make the top right box something like 65 and the total 88. But if the student puts 23 in the top right or the bottom, the numbers are likely to be different. Students could experiment with putting the 23 (or other numbers) in each of the possible boxes.

> Fill in one of the boxes with the number 23.
>
> Consider how long the boxes are.
>
> Then put other numbers in the other boxes that make sense.

[*Possible solutions:* 23, 65, 88, or 8, 23, 31, or 6, 17, 23.]

➤ Students are empowered when they get to make their own choices. In the task below, they also get to interpret what "fairly large" and "fairly small" mean. Mathematically, a task like this one helps students see that adding larger values gives a greater sum, but if both values are larger, the difference might actually be smaller.

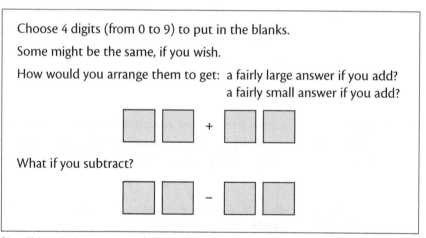

> Choose 4 digits (from 0 to 9) to put in the blanks.
>
> Some might be the same, if you wish.
>
> How would you arrange them to get: a fairly large answer if you add?
>   a fairly small answer if you add?
>
> What if you subtract?

[*Possible solutions:* Large if you add: 99 + 99; small if you add: 10 + 10; large if you subtract: 99 − 10; small if you subtract: 44 − 42.]

> Students do not really engage in full-blown multiplication in Grade 2, but some activities to get them started thinking about numbers that are groups of 2 (i.e., even numbers), doubles, and arrays include the following:

> You can add a LOT of 2s to model a number.
>
> What might the number be? How many 2s would you need?

[*Solution:* Any even number; half of it tells how many 2s are needed.]

OR

> Put 5 square tiles in a line. Put a mirror at the end of the line.
>
> How many square tiles do you see now (include the original tiles and the images)? Why does that make sense?
>
> Where could you put the mirror so you see a total of 6 tiles?

[*Solution:* 10 squares, because there are 2 sets of 5; put the mirror after the dark 3rd square to see only 6.]

OR

> Choose some counters.
>
> Arrange them into 6 equal-length rows.
>
> How many counters might you have?

Suggestions for Home Activities: 2nd Grade

You might encourage parents to come to school for a "fun math at home" program or create short videos for them and post them on your school website. Make sure parents are familiar with and comfortable with the kinds of math activities their children are performing in school. You might also create a blog with short postings or videos where you model or talk about some of the math activities in which their children are engaging.

> Encourage parents to find opportunities at the grocery store with their child to add money amounts under $1.

➤ Encourage parents to ask their children to determine interesting totals in the house. For example: How many knives, forks, and spoons are on the dinner table? How many are there altogether?

➤ Encourage parents to solve appropriate math problems with their children. A good source is: http://figurethis.nctm.org

➤ Parents might ask their children to identify words worth between 40 and 60 if A = 1, B = 2, C = 3, . . . , and Z = 26. [*Possible words:* tot, tire, sat, sit, top, roar.]

➤ Encourage parents to play math games with their children at home. They might invent their own games involving addition or subtraction, or they might use games like these or adaptations of them.

Close to 20

Two players play.

Each player rolls two dice to get a 2-digit number twice.

The player determines the difference.

The difference closest to 20 wins a point.

The first person to reach 10 points wins the game.

Four Cards

The game uses a shuffled deck with four sets of cards numbered 1 to 10 (40 cards altogether).

Two players play.

Each player chooses four cards from the deck.

The player adds all the values. He or she gets a point if the total is more than 25.

The player then subtracts the least value from the greatest and gets a point if the difference is exactly 4.

The first player with 25 points wins the game.

❖ CHAPTER 4 ❖

Number and Operations in Base Ten

THIS CHAPTER focuses on ideas related to place value and operations that are built on place value concepts.

THE FUNDAMENTALS

Place Value

Two fundamental concepts underlie our place value system.

The first of these concepts is that we use only 10 digits, 0 to 9, to represent all numbers, and the placement of a digit within a numeral reflects its intended value. For example, the 2 in 12 represents 2 ones, whereas the 2 in 21 represents 2 tens and the 2 in 200 represents 2 hundreds.

The second concept, which is related to the first, is that we use a 10-for-1 trading system when writing numerals. That is, when we have 10 ones or 10 tens, and we are recording the number symbolically, we trade them for 1 ten or 1 hundred, respectively. For example, adding 13 to 28 results in a total of 3 tens and 11 ones, but this is not written as 311. Instead, we trade 10 ones for another ten and write 41. Notice that the trading is required only to write the number symbolically; physically, we can have 10 or more ones or 10 or more tens.

Manipulatives Used for Representing 2-Digit and 3-Digit Numbers

➤ Ten-Frames

Ten-frames are a useful tool for young students. The tens digit of a number tells how many full ten-frames are used. The ones digit tells how many counters are in the last, unfilled ten-frame, if there is an unfilled frame.

For example, 17 is 1 ten and 7 ones and is represented with 1 full ten-frame and 7 counters in the last, unfilled frame:

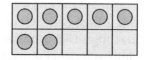

This kind of representation is one of students' earlier experiences with what we call **unitizing**, that is, counting a group of items as one item. In this case, the 10 counters in the full ten-frame constitute 1 group of ten.

Students might be asked a question like this to test their understanding of ten-frame use:

How many counters do I need to fill a ten-frame and half of another one?

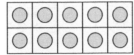 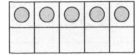

> ### Unifix or Linking Cubes

Students might use chains (or trains or sticks) of 10 **unifix** or **linking cubes**; a single train represents 1 ten. Other cubes can be either loose or in a train (but not in a train of 10). For example, 23 is made up of 2 trains of 10 unifix cubes and another 3 cubes:

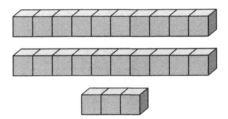

You might ask a question like this of your students:

How many cubes are there if there is 1 stick of 10 cubes and another 6 cubes?

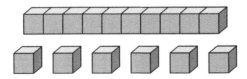

➤ *Bags of Buttons*

Students might use small bags that hold 10 buttons, along with loose buttons, to represent numbers. For example, 36 can be represented by using 3 small bags, each holding 10 buttons, and then 6 more buttons:

It is important that students realize that when we write a number of the form 1☐—such as 12, 15, 18—we mean 10 + ☐. Often they meet these numbers, especially 10, before they realize this. So you might use activities like the ones below to help students come to this understanding:

How many buttons are there in 1 full bag of 10 and 2 more buttons?

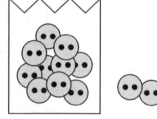

Fill in the box with a number less than 10.

Then say what the triangle number is.

Use other numbers less than 10 for the box, too.

$$10 + \square = \triangle$$

Choose a number between 10 and 20.

Represent it in a way that makes it easy to see how much more than 10 it is.

> ## Base-Ten Blocks

All of the materials described thus far are good for starting work with tens and ones because students can easily put together 10 items to make a unit of ten or decompose a ten into 10 ones. Eventually, as they begin to work with larger numbers, students are likely to use **base-ten blocks**.

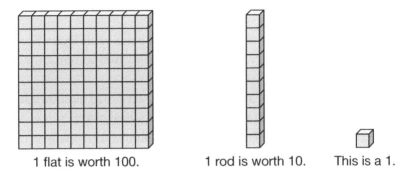

1 flat is worth 100.   1 rod is worth 10.   This is a 1.

A student might show 143 as 1 flat, 4 rods, and 3 ones:

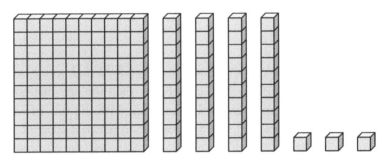

Alternatively, the student could use 14 tens and 3 ones to represent 143:

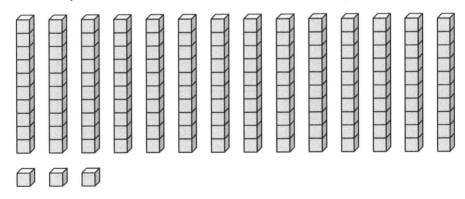

With base-ten blocks, the materials are still proportional: a ten still looks as big as 10 ones, and a hundred looks like 10 tens. But students cannot literally take apart a 10-rod to make 10 ones; they can only line up 10 ones to see that they are the same length as the rod. Similarly, students cannot literally take apart a 100-flat to make 10 rods; they can only line up 10 rods to see that they are the same size as the flat.

Materials like base-ten blocks should be used later than the ones described earlier. However, base-ten blocks become convenient since they don't take as much work as creating unifix trains, counting out all the counters to fill ten-frames, or making lots of bags of 10 buttons, and they certainly make it easier to show numbers that are 3 digits or more.

➤ Later "Concrete" Models

At some point, students are likely to use a **place value chart** like the one shown below, but in the primary grades it is probably best to remain with proportional materials such as those described earlier.

For example, later, a student might represent 324 as shown here. Notice that with a place value chart rather than proportional materials, it is easy for students to forget that the 2 counters in the middle column are actually worth 20 and not 2.

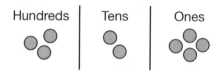

➤ The 100-Chart

The 100-chart is useful for representing, visually, 2-digit numbers. The form of the chart that goes from 0 to 99 is even better than the one that goes from 1 to 100 because students can connect the tens digit with the row in which the number appears and the ones digit with the column in which it appears. For example, any number with a tens digit of 5 is in the same row and any number with a ones digit of 5 is in the same column.

0	1	2	3	4	5	6	7	8	9
10	11	12	13	14	15	16	17	18	19
20	21	22	23	24	25	26	27	28	29
30	31	32	33	34	35	36	37	38	39
40	41	42	43	44	45	46	47	48	49
50	51	52	53	54	55	56	57	58	59
60	61	62	63	64	65	66	67	68	69
70	71	72	73	74	75	76	77	78	79
80	81	82	83	84	85	86	87	88	89
90	91	92	93	94	95	96	97	98	99

The Number Line

Once students are comfortable skip counting by 10s or 100s, they might use number lines to represent 2-digit and 3-digit numbers. For example, 73 is represented as a little past 70 or 212 as not too much past 200.

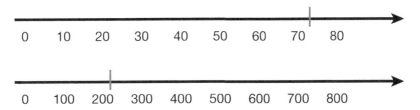

Representing 2-Digit and 3-Digit Numbers

Students often learn to write the numeral 10 long before they learn the place value concepts that help them understand that this is a way of representing a tens column in the place value chart and that what we are really talking about is 1 ten and 0 ones. Introducing 100 as meaning 1 hundred will require discussion of a new column in the place value chart that describes groups of 10 tens.

A variety of concrete models for representing 2-digit and 3-digit numbers were described earlier. What matters mathematically is that students are flexible in representing these greater numbers.

For example, we want students to realize that the number 43 could be represented with place value materials as 4 tens and 3 ones, or as 3 tens and 13 ones, or as 2 tens and 23 ones, or as 1 ten and 33 ones, or even as 43 ones.

Similarly, 128 is 1 hundred, 2 tens, and 8 ones, or 12 tens and 8 ones, or 1 hundred and 28 ones, or 11 tens and 18 ones, and so forth.

Without that flexibility, students will not be as successful with adding and subtracting or comparing numbers as they could be with a good grasp of this concept.

To reinforce the fact that digit placement affects digit value, you might use a question like the one below. The digits 2 and 3 are arbitrary, and students could choose their own digits instead if they wish. Or you can use the question repeatedly with different digit pairs.

> Use the digits 2 and 3 to make two different 2-digit numbers.
>
> Tell as many things as you can about the two numbers.
>
> Tell which is more and how you know that.

Estimation

Students benefit from experiences where they estimate quantities relative to more familiar numbers, such as multiples of 10 or 100.

The estimation might also be physical. For example, if the small container at the left holds 10 counters, students might estimate the number of counters that would fit in the containers on the right:

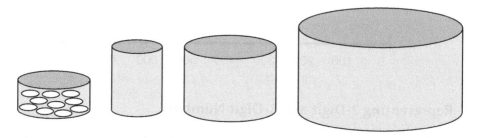

Students will also estimate in strictly numerical, not physical, situations. This is done, for example, when placing numbers on a number line. They might estimate 42 as being around 40 (just 2 more) or around 50 (not even 10 less), depending on the scale of the number line. Rather than focusing on rules for rounding, estimation should be contextually based when context is involved, and estimates should just make sense.

Comparing 2-Digit and 3-Digit Numbers

Rather than just teaching students rules for comparing 2-digit and 3-digit numbers, it is important that they understand why one number is greater than another.

Fundamentally, one whole number is greater than another if it comes later in the counting sequence: 1, 2, 3, 4, ... Certainly we do not want students to count from 1 for great numbers, but this idea is an important one to hold, and it is useful for smaller numbers, even up to 20 or 30.

We might want students to think about **benchmarks**, probably multiples of 10 or 100, to help them compare numbers. First they need to realize that □ tens is more than △ tens if □ is more than △; the same idea works for hundreds. Then students might start thinking like this:

- 23 < 45 since 23 is less than 3 tens and 45 is more than 4 tens, and 3 tens is less than 4 tens.
- 341 > 189 since 341 is more than 3 hundreds and 189 is not even 2 hundreds, and 3 hundreds is more than 2 hundreds.

When we teach students, with 2-digit numbers, to look at only the tens digits to compare them—for example, when comparing 47 and 61—we are simply giving them a quick way to say that 47 is not even 5 tens and 61 is more than 6 tens. This method works not because 60 is more than 40; in fact, 47 is also more than 40, just not as much more as 60 is. It works because 47 is not more than 50, and 60 is more than 50.

Visually, students might compare 2-digit numbers by, for example, looking at both numbers represented on ten-frames, matching counters one-to-one, to see which uses more counters.

Or students might compare base-ten blocks in a one-to-one way. For example, this model shows that 216 is more than 190:

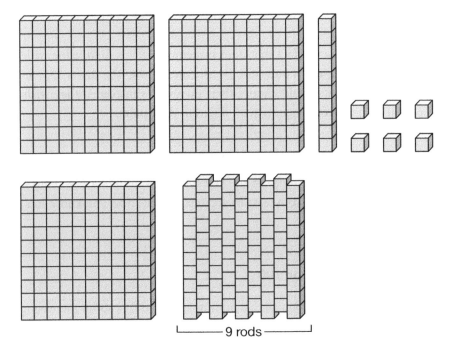

—— 9 rods ——

The student might even put the pieces from 190 on top of the pieces from 216 to demonstrate that some parts of 216 are uncovered, so it must be greater.

Students might also use estimation to compare two numbers, particularly when the numbers are not close. For example, 234 > 158 since 234 is about 23 tens and 168 is about 16 tens, and 23 is more than 16.

Rather than directly asking students to look at two numbers to decide which is more, it is more instructive to have them incorporate some probabilistic thinking, as is required in the activities at top of the next page. They will realize that sometimes you can be sure which is greater (even without all the digits)—for example, 3☐ must be less than 4☐ no matter what numbers are in the boxes—but at other times you cannot be certain.

How sure are you about which number is greater each time? Explain.

3☐ *and* 4☐   3☐ *and* ☐3

5☐ *and* ☐4

For older students, you might use larger numbers, for example:

How sure are you about which number is greater each time? Explain.

3☐☐ *and* 4☐☐   3☐4 *and* 6☐3

5☐3 *and* ☐24

To reinforce the fact that digit placement affects digit value with larger numbers, you might use a question like the one below. The digits 4, 5, and 6 are arbitrary, so students could choose their own digits instead if they wish. Or you can use the question repeatedly with different digit pairs.

Use the digits 4, 5, and 6 to make different 3-digit numbers.

Tell as many things as you can about the numbers you created.

Order them from least to greatest and tell how you know you are right.

Mentally Adding 10 or 100

Students need to recognize that adding 10 (or 100) is about increasing the tens (or hundreds) digit by 1 since there is 1 extra ten (or hundred). There should be no need for use of paper and pencil.

It makes sense that if you have, for example, 2 hundreds, 1 ten, and 4 ones (214), an extra ten would make 2 hundreds, 2 tens, and 4 ones (224) or an extra hundred would make 3 hundreds but would not affect the tens and ones (314).

The 100-chart makes this easy to see when adding 10 to a 2-digit number. Adding 10 means going down 1 row, so the tens digit is 1 more and the ones digit does not change.

0	1	2	3	4	5	6	7	8	9
10	11	12	13	14	15	16	17	18	19
20	21	22	23	24	25	26	27	28	29
30	31	32	33	34	35	36	37	38	39
40	41	42	43	44	45	46	47	48	49
50	51	52	53	54	55	56	57	58	59
60	61	62	63	64	65	66	67	68	69
70	71	72	73	74	75	76	77	78	79
80	81	82	83	84	85	86	87	88	89
90	91	92	93	94	95	96	97	98	99

Not only do we want students to be able to figure out the number that is 10 more or 10 less than another number, we want them to understand why this is not a difficult task. You might use activities like these:

Choose a 2-digit number.

Now tell the number that is 10 more and the number that is 10 less.

Tell why this was not too hard to do.

Choose a 3-digit number.

Now tell the numbers that are 10 more and 10 less and 100 more and 100 less.

Tell why this was not too hard to do.

Skip Counting by 5s, 10s, and 100s

Skip counting by 10s and 100s is really all about place value. If skip counting by 10s or 100s comes first, then mentally adding 10 and 100 becomes easy—it is just the next number in the skip count. If, instead, mental addition of 10 or 100 comes first, then skip counting involves repeatedly using that skill.

Skip counting by 5s is somewhat different. Usually students first skip count by 5s starting at 5, then starting at a multiple of 5, and only later starting anywhere. Normally students observe patterns based on repeatedly adding 5: they notice that there are only two ones digits in the numbers in the pattern and that the tens value changes after 2 skips.

For example, if we start at 35, the numbers go 35, 40, 45, 50, 55, 60, ... The only ones digits are 0 and 5. It makes sense that adding 5 twice is the same as adding 10, so the tens digit increases after two skips but the ones digit does not change.

If we start at 38, the numbers go 38, 43, 48, 53, 58, 63, 68, ... Again, there are only two ones digits: 3 and 8. Again, the tens digit changes after two skips.

Adding a 1-Digit Number to a 2-Digit Number

Students are likely to—and should be encouraged to—use the same strategies they learned to add with small numbers when they add 1-digit numbers to 2-digit numbers.

For example, to add 43 + 9, a student might use compensation by adding 10 and then subtracting 1 to compensate for having added too much: 43 + 9 = 43 + 10 − 1 = 52.

Or a student might use the associative property of addition and move 1 over from the 43 to the 9: 43 is 42 + 1, so move the 1 over to the 9 (to make 10) and add 42 + 10 to get 52.

Or a student might use the associative property in a different way: 9 is 7 + 2, so first add 7 to the 43 to get 50, and then add 2 more to get 52.

Students might model these actions using concrete manipulatives, visual tools such as the 100-chart, or a number line. The number line might have tick marks and numerals already indicated, or it might be an **open number line**, where students select which numbers are critical to identify for the purpose at hand.

➤ Using Ten-Frames

To add 43 + 9, start with 4 full ten-frames and a frame with only 3 counters (to represent 43) as well as a frame showing 9 counters:

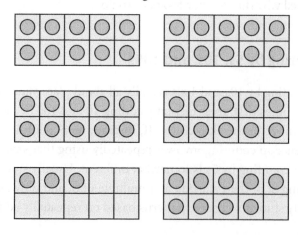

Then, 7 counters are moved over to fill the fifth ten-frame, leaving only 2 counters in the last frame, representing the total of 52:

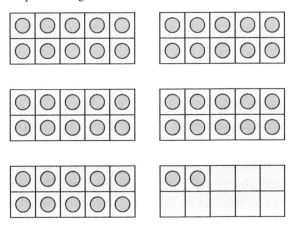

> ## ➤ Using the 100-Chart

To add 43 + 9 on the 100-chart, start at 43, go down 1 row to 53 (to add 10) and then move back 1 (to compensate):

0	1	2	3	4	5	6	7	8	9
10	11	12	13	14	15	16	17	18	19
20	21	22	23	24	25	26	27	28	29
30	31	32	33	34	35	36	37	38	39
40	41	42	43	44	45	46	47	48	49
50	51	52	53	54	55	56	57	58	59
60	61	62	63	64	65	66	67	68	69
70	71	72	73	74	75	76	77	78	79
80	81	82	83	84	85	86	87	88	89
90	91	92	93	94	95	96	97	98	99

> ## ➤ Using the Open Number Line

To add 43 + 9 on the open number line, you might add 7 and then 2 more, marking 43, 50, and 52 on the number line:

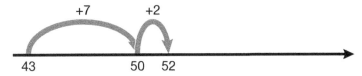

Subtracting a 1-Digit Number from a 2-Digit Number

Similarly, a student can use the strategies and properties of subtraction that were used to work with smaller numbers to subtract 1-digit numbers from 2-digit numbers.

For example, when thinking about 46 – 3, a student might use a variation of the associative property to think of this as 40 + 6 – 3 and move the 6 over to the –3. That student thinks that there is 40 and then 6 – 3, or 3, so the result is 43.

When thinking about 43 – 6, a student might subtract only 3 and then compensate by subtracting the rest of the 6, that is, another 3. So, the process begins as 43 – 3 = 40 and then continues with 40 – 3 = 37 (counting back 3 from 40). Or the student might change the problem to 46 – 6 and then compensate for adding the extra 3 to 43 by subtracting that extra 3 from the result of the modified problem. Or a student might subtract 10 instead of 6, and then add back the extra 4 she or he subtracted: 43 – 10 = 33 and 33 + 4 = 37.

Again, concrete models such as ten-frames, the 100-chart, or open number lines can be used. The examples that follow show how these tools might be used to perform the subtraction 51 – 8.

➤ Using Ten-Frames

Subtracting 51 – 8 by using ten-frames begins by representing 51 as 5 full ten-frames and a frame with 1 counter:

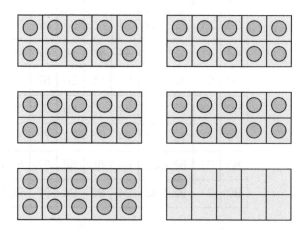

Then, to subtract 8, a student might remove a whole ten-frame and add back 2 counters. That would result in 4 full ten-frames and 3 counters, as shown on the next page:

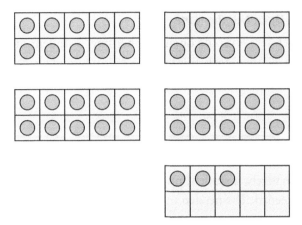

> ## Using the 100-Chart

To subtract 51 – 8 on the 100-chart, you might start at 51 and subtract 10 by going up a row to 41, and then compensate by adding back 2 (moving 2 to the right) to get to 43. Alternatively, students could mark both 8 and 51 and count how many spaces they need to move to get from one to the other. Since the movement is 4 rows down and another 3 numbers, the result is 43.

0	1	2	3	4	5	6	7	8	9
10	11	12	13	14	15	16	17	18	19
20	21	22	23	24	25	26	27	28	29
30	31	32	33	34	35	36	37	38	39
40	41	42	43	44	45	46	47	48	49
50	51	52	53	54	55	56	57	58	59
60	61	62	63	64	65	66	67	68	69
70	71	72	73	74	75	76	77	78	79
80	81	82	83	84	85	86	87	88	89
90	91	92	93	94	95	96	97	98	99

> ## *Using the Open Number Line*

To subtract 51 − 8 on the open number line, a student might begin at 51, go back 1 to get to 50, then back another 5 to 45, and finally back another 2 to reach 43:

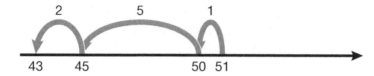

Alternatively, a student might start at 8 and go up to 51 and count how big a move is needed. The needed moves total 43:

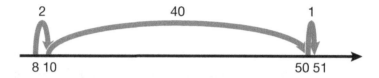

Adding or Subtracting Multiples of 10 or Multiples of 100

It is important for students to understand that adding 2 tens to 3 tens or 2 hundreds to 3 hundreds is just like adding 2 bananas to 3 bananas. As long as the units are the same, 2 of something and 3 of that same thing makes 5 of that thing. So, 2 tens + 3 tens = 5 tens, and 2 hundreds + 3 hundreds = 5 hundreds.

Seeing the expression 500 + 300, a student thinks this is 5 hundreds + 3 hundreds, or 5 + 3 hundreds.

These ideas are stronger ones for students to call on than having them simply follow a procedure and line up numbers in columns and add 0s and 2 and 3.

Students should also understand that 5 tens + 3 hundreds is neither 8 tens nor 8 hundreds (since the units are different). To make the units the same, they might think of 3 hundreds as 30 tens and then add 5 tens + 30 tens.

Visually, students can see that if they combine 5 flats with 3 flats, there are 8 flats:

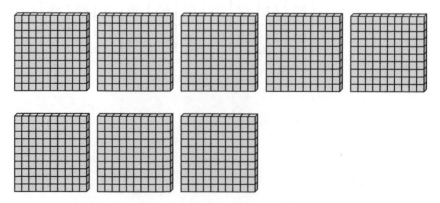

It is essential for students to consider alternative strategies they might employ to do a variety of appropriate calculations. You can strengthen the task suggested below by asking students to think of other questions for which they would use the same strategies.

What strategy would you use to do each calculation?	
25 + 8	29 + 6
43 + 8	50 – 20
43 + 80	

Adding 2-Digit Numbers or 3-Digit Numbers

Students continue to apply the same strategies learned earlier to add either two 2-digit numbers, two 3-digit numbers, or a 3-digit number and a 2-digit number. Using ten-frames or the 100-chart is practical for 2-digit numbers, although less practical for 3-digit numbers or sums that are 3-digit numbers. Using base-ten blocks works well for either sort of number. The underlying ideas, though, are the same no matter what the numbers are.

Students should be encouraged to come up with personal strategies for adding numbers, using visual support if they wish. To illustrate, some different ways students might consider adding 48 + 37, 153 + 287, and 312 + 49 are described.

➤ 48 + 37

One student might add 50 + 37, knowing that result is 8 tens and 7 ones, and then compensate by removing the extra 2 added by using 50 instead of 48, to get 85.

Another student might take advantage of the associative property and move 2 over from 37 to 48 and then add 50 + 35 to get 85.

Another student might add 40 + 30 to get 70, and 8 + 7 to get 15, for a total of 85.

Another student might use the 100-chart. She or he could start at 48, move down 4 to add 40 (arriving at 88), and then compensate by moving back 3 to get to 85:

0	1	2	3	4	5	6	7	8	9
10	11	12	13	14	15	16	17	18	19
20	21	22	23	24	25	26	27	28	29
30	31	32	33	34	35	36	37	38	39
40	41	42	43	44	45	46	47	48	49
50	51	52	53	54	55	56	57	58	59
60	61	62	63	64	65	66	67	68	69
70	71	72	73	74	75	76	77	78	79
80	81	82	83	84	85	86	87	88	89
90	91	92	93	94	95	96	97	98	99

Another student might use base-ten blocks by showing 37 and then adding 5 rods (50 instead of 48) and removing 2 ones to compensate.

Another student might use an open number line like this:

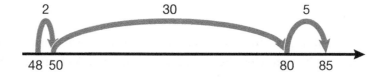

153 + 287

At this developmental level, students are likely to use concrete materials for this question. Students might model both numbers, put them together, and do any trading required.

In this case, the student could use base-ten blocks to model 153 and 287 separately. He or she would see that there are 3 hundreds, 13 tens, and 10 ones (as shown on the next page), which can be traded for 4 hundreds, 3 tens, and 10 ones, which can then be traded for 4 hundreds, 4 tens, and 0 ones. The result is 440.

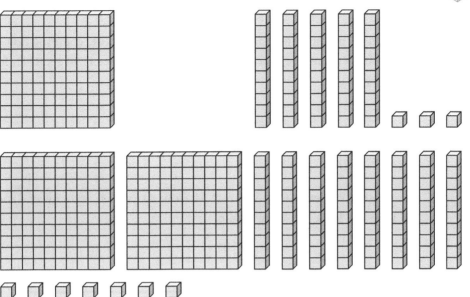

Or the student might model 287 first. To add 153, she or he might add a flat, next add 2 rods and trade the resulting 10 rods for another flat, then add the other 3 rods, and finally add 3 ones, trading for another rod.

Some students might use open number lines, but most students benefit from working with concrete materials at this level.

➤ *312 + 49*

Students might use base-ten blocks to model 312 and then add 5 rods and remove 1 one. This describes adding 50 and then removing 1 to compensate.

Or the student might begin with the same model of 312, and then add 4 rods and 9 ones. Next 10 of the ones could be traded for another rod, resulting in a total of 3 flats, 6 rods, and 1 one, or 361.

Subtracting 2-Digit Numbers or 3-Digit Numbers

Students continue the same strategies learned earlier with smaller numbers to subtract either two 2-digit numbers, two 3-digit numbers, or a 2-digit number from a 3-digit number. Again, using ten-frames or the 100-chart is practical for 2-digit numbers, although less practical for 3-digit numbers. Using base-ten blocks works well for either sort of number.

Students should be encouraged to come up with personal strategies for subtracting numbers, using visual support if they wish. Following are shown some different ways students might consider calculating 41 – 27, 312 – 176, or 173 – 77.

> *41 – 27*

One student might think about adding up from 27 to 41, counting how much is added. That student might add 3 to get to 30 and another 11 to get to 41, for a total difference of 14.

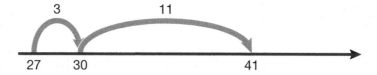

Another student might subtract 31 from 41 (which takes away 4 too many) and then add back 4 to compensate.

Another student might subtract 27 from 41 in three steps: take away 20 from 41 to get to 21, then subtract 1 to get to 20, and then subtract the remaining 6 to get to 14.

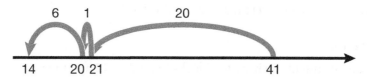

Using the 100-chart, another student might start at 41, move up 3 (subtracting 30) to get to 11, and move right to add back 3 to compensate since too much was subtracted to start. Alternatively, the student might start at 27 and notice the need to count 10 and another 4 to get to 41, for a missing addend of 14.

0	1	2	3	4	5	6	7	8	9
10	11	12	13	14	15	16	17	18	19
20	21	22	23	24	25	26	27	28	29
30	31	32	33	34	35	36	37	38	39
40	41	42	43	44	45	46	47	48	49
50	51	52	53	54	55	56	57	58	59
60	61	62	63	64	65	66	67	68	69
70	71	72	73	74	75	76	77	78	79
80	81	82	83	84	85	86	87	88	89
90	91	92	93	94	95	96	97	98	99

Yet another student might use base-ten blocks by modeling 41 and covering those blocks with 27, counting how much is left uncovered. In this case, it is 3 ones plus 1 ten and another one, for a total of 14 uncovered.

Another student might use an open number line like this one, observing the need for a total move of 14.

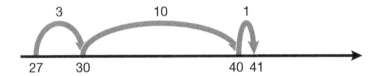

➤ 312 – 176

At this level, students are likely to use concrete materials for subtracting 3-digit numbers, most likely base-ten blocks.

One student might model 312, cover up 176 of it with more blocks, and see what's left. In this case, 100 + 30 + 6, or 136, remains uncovered, as shown on the next page.

Other students might model 312 and realize they need to remove more ones and tens than they have. So they might trade 1 hundred for 10 tens and 1 ten for 10 ones.

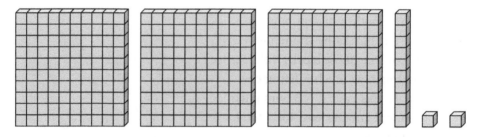

After these trades, 312 becomes the following:

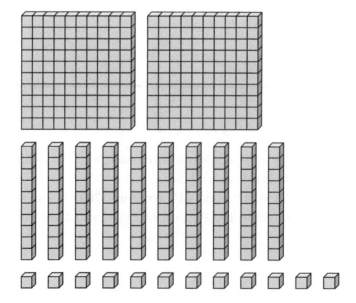

Then 1 flat, 7 rods, and 6 ones are removed, leaving 136.

Or a student might show 176 and count how much more is needed to make 312 (looking for the missing addend):

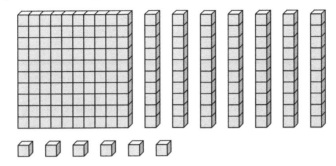

The student needs 4 more to get to 180, 20 more to get to 200, and then 112 more to get to 312, for a total addition of 136.

➤ 173 – 77

Some students will figure out that 177 – 77 = 100 and simply subtract 4 more to compensate for the 4 they added to 173 to get to 177. They count back 4 to 96.

Students who use base-ten blocks might cover 173 with 77 to see how much is left uncovered. Or they might trade the hundred flat for 10 ten rods and 1 rod for 10 ones and then remove 7 rods and 7 ones, leaving 9 rods and 6 ones.

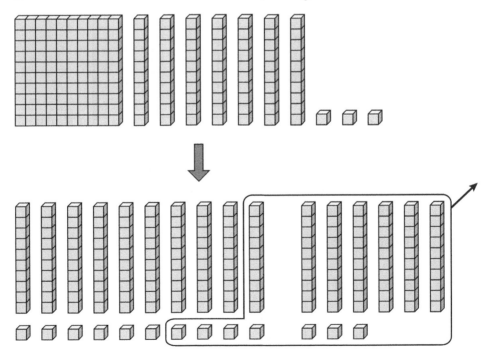

Using the number line, students might add on from 77. By adding 3 to get to 80, 20 to get to 100, and then 73 more, there is a total addition of 96.

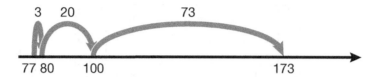

It is valuable for students to consider alternative strategies they might employ to do a variety of calculations. You can strengthen the task by asking students to think of other questions for which they would use the same strategies.

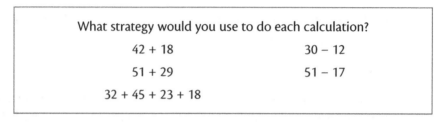

What strategy would you use to do each calculation?

42 + 18	30 − 12
51 + 29	51 − 17
32 + 45 + 23 + 18	

Alternatively, you might use a task like this one and vary it to provide lots of insightful practice:

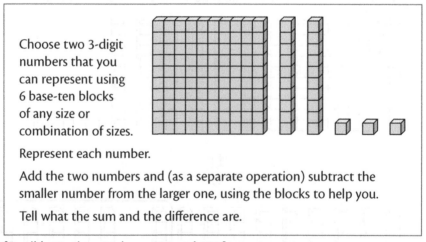

Choose two 3-digit numbers that you can represent using 6 base-ten blocks of any size or combination of sizes.

Represent each number.

Add the two numbers and (as a separate operation) subtract the smaller number from the larger one, using the blocks to help you.

Tell what the sum and the difference are.

[*Possible starting numbers:* 330 and 123.]

The Importance of Estimation

It is important for students to estimate to see whether their calculated answers seem reasonable or perhaps because an estimate is all that is required. Rounding is only one form of estimation; there are always many ways to estimate.

For example, to estimate 344 + 263, a student might think any of these ways:

- About 300 + 300 is about 600.
- About 300 + 250 is about 550.
- About 350 + 250 is about 500 + 100 = 600.
- Between 500 (300 + 200) and 700 (400 + 300) is about 600.

Students are often reluctant to estimate when there is too much emphasis on getting the exact right answer. Consider whether you are overemphasizing this or not. Let students know when an estimate will be sufficient.

MISCONCEPTIONS TO WATCH FOR

➢ *Symbolizing Teen Numbers Incorrectly.* Many children will choose to write, for example, 61 rather than 16 to represent sixteen, since they hear the 6 first. It is only through many exposures to our convention of writing the 1 first that students will internalize how we write teen numbers.

For many of these students, it will be once they meet other 2-digit numbers involving 20s, 30s, and so forth, when it starts to make sense that the 1 comes first for the teen numbers because it will be consistent with the first digit telling how many tens.

➢ *Misunderstanding Teen Numbers.* Some children will think of 14 as 1 and 4 (or 5) rather than as 10 and 4. Be consistent in saying 10 and 4, or fourteen, and be careful not to ever say 1 and 4.

➢ *Symbolizing 2-Digit and 3-Digit Numbers Incorrectly.* Many students write, symbolically, what they hear. When they hear twenty-four, they might write 204, knowing that the twenty part is written 20; similarly, they might write 3005 for three hundred five.

➢ *Misapplying Strategies for Addition or Subtraction.* Many students will compensate incorrectly when they use strategies to add or subtract. For example, when working out 23 + 38 by adding 40 instead of 38, they might add an extra 2 at the end rather than subtracting it; in their minds, they are doing an addition question and they think only about adding.

Similarly, when working out 305 – 187 by subtracting 200 from 305, they might subtract the 13 difference rather than adding it back at the end.

THE FUN

Pre-K and Kindergarten

These activities provide engaging learning and practice opportunities. There are not a lot of activities for the pre-K–kindergarten age group, because content in Number and Operations in Base Ten does not become a significant part of the curriculum until 1st grade.

➤ Students might practice thinking about teen numbers as 1 group of ten and some ones by using the following activities:

Throw three bean bags at a big mat that looks like this.		
Read the number you land on each time.		
Tell how much more than 10 it is.		

18	13	19
16	14	15
11	12	17

OR

The activity below has the advantage of providing practice with teen numbers, and at the same time students have opportunities to develop estimation skills. This activity uses counters but could be done with anything students might find interesting, such as marbles, beads, Lego-type blocks, paper clips, or pennies.

> Laila said that when she reaches into a jar of counters, she usually can grab between 10 and 20 at a time with one hand.
>
> Check Laila's idea.
>
> Record the number of counters you get.

➤ The activity at the top of the next page is interesting to students because they always love using their names.

Asking them about whether the first name can have 10 letters alerts students to quantity in their lives. Asking about the number of letters in the last name helps them notice that if 10 is removed from $10 + \square$, what is left is $\square$.

> Choose a number between 10 and 20.
>
> Make up a first and last name with that many letters altogether.
>
> Could the first name have 10 letters?
>
> If it did, how many letters would the last name need to have?

[*Possible solutions:* Laura Stevens or Christiane Ng for 12 letters.]

OR

The activity below is fun for students because they get to paint or color. Asking students how they determined how many circles would be the second color helps them focus on the math involved in the task.

> Choose a number between 10 and 20. You will paint that many circles.
>
> Paint 10 circles a color you like.
>
> Paint the rest of the circles a different color you like.
>
> How did you know how many circles you needed to paint the second color?
>
> Make a picture with your circles.

Suggestions for Home Activities: Pre-K and Kindergarten

Let parents know that their children are working on getting familiar with the notion that the numbers from 10–19 are all numbers that are 10 and some more, but not 2 tens.

> Encourage parents to find opportunities to talk about teen numbers (e.g., ages of cousins or siblings, the number of pieces of silverware on the table, house numbers, etc.) with their children to help them become familiar with those numbers.

> Ask parents to make sure not to say that, for example, 13 is 1 and 3, but to say that it's 10 and 3.

> Suggest to parents that they might access the book *Meet the Teens* (Cooper, 2011) and read it with their children.

1st Grade

These activities provide engaging learning and practice opportunities.

Note: Some activities described in the previous chapter on Operations and Algebraic Thinking might apply to the Number and Operations in Base Ten standards as well.

➤ Students are expected to be able to count to 120 from any number. Rolling dice makes the starting point more random. Counting 20 numbers, as requested in the task below, is just a way to ask students to continue to count. They could have been asked, instead, to count up to 100 or up to 120 or to count another 30 numbers or 10 numbers.

> Roll two dice.
> One number tells how many tens.
> The other number tells how many ones.
> Start at that number and count 20 more numbers.

➤ Students need practice in hearing how we read and write the multiples of 10. The suggested activity below is an unusual, but interesting, way to practice. It turns out that 20, 30, 40, . . . , and so on, are all words that end with the letters "ty." Before the "ty" are either 3, 4, or 5 letters.

> Spin a spinner that looks like this:
>
>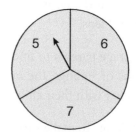
>
> Then say a number word with that many letters that ends in "ty" and write the number as a number.

[*Solutions:* 5 letters: forty, fifty, sixty; 6 letters: twenty, thirty, eighty, ninety; 7 letters: seventy]

➤ You might prepare laminated minivans based on ten-frames for students to use. If you feel it will bother students for the vans not to have drivers, you can put a picture of a driver in the front part of each van. You might suggest students try a lot of different numbers.

Choose one of these numbers of kids who are going on an outing:
30, 40, 50, 60, 70, 80, 90, or 100 kids.

If a ten-frame van holds 10 kids,
and there are no empty seats,
how many vans will you need?

Some students might want their vans to carry different numbers of kids (e.g.,
25) and not just multiples of 10. Let that happen if students wish.

> Students need practice representing 2-digit numbers. Using the activity below
involves physical activity as well as representing numbers.

Drop three beanbags on a big mat
like this one.

Represent each number you land on
by using ten-frames or base-ten
blocks.

86	65	34	95	27
13	79	86	36	60
15	23	33	46	92
76	57	92	71	99
50	43	52	67	48

OR

In the activity below, students enjoy the unpredictability of what numbers of fingers will be put up. Because of this unpredictability, students can get lots of practice by reusing the activity or taking multiple turns.

Play with a partner.

Model your numbers with blocks.

One of you puts out 1, 2, or 3 fingers.

Show that many tens.

The other puts out 3, 4, or 5 fingers.

Show that many ones.

Write the number you made.

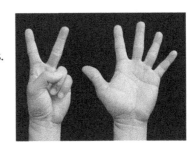

OR

Double tap some children and single tap some other children to begin the activity below. This allows for a separate tens digit and ones digit. Students will enjoy being tapped and, again, there is an exciting element of unpredictability. The rest of the class (non-tapped children) should answer the last question.

> If you were tapped twice, come up front and hold up ALL 10 of your fingers.
>
> If you were tapped once, come up and hold up 1 finger.
>
> How many fingers are up?

> Students need to learn that a number with more tens (assuming there are 9 or fewer ones) is a greater number. They need many experiences to internalize this. One way to set up this learning is by using coins, as suggested below, where dimes represent tens and pennies represent ones. (In Canada, where pennies are no longer produced, plastic pennies might be used.) To reinforce the idea that a number with more tens is worth more (assuming fewer than 10 pennies in each number), once students have represented their numbers and told how many cents, you might ask: *Is it worth more if you have more dimes or more pennies? How come?*

> Play with a partner.
>
> Each of you:
>
>
>
> - Rolls a die to decide how many dimes you get.
> - Rolls another die to decide how many pennies you get.
>
> Show your number.
>
>
>
> Write how many cents it is.
>
> Whose amount is worth more?

OR

Students will enjoy creating toothpick pictures. Math is at play in this activity both when they represent the numbers they used each time and when they figure out how to ensure that their second picture uses more toothpicks. It is important to observe what strategies students use to compare: Do they use unsophisticated strategies such as matching 1-1, or do they recognize that the same number of tens and more ones or more tens ensures more toothpicks?

Grab more than 20 toothpicks.

Make a picture with many or all the toothpicks and tell how many you used.

Now make a picture with more toothpicks.

Tell how many you used this time.

How do you know the second amount is more?

OR

Prepare cards with 2-digit numbers on one side. Give groups of 3 students a small pack of these cards. You can turn this activity into a competition by suggesting that a student who guesses correctly gets a point. The first child to 10 points wins. There is some element of probability involved since you can never (or almost never) be sure whether you have the greatest, the least, or the middle number. But the activity does encourage mathematical reasoning. For example, a number like 92 is a good bet for greatest; a number like 12 is a good bet for least; a number like 43 is a good bet for middle.

Use a deck of cards with 2-digit numbers.

Play in 3s.

Each of you takes a card.

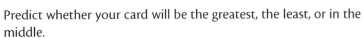

34   81   27

Do not show it to the others.

Predict whether your card will be the greatest, the least, or in the middle.

Check to see if you are right.

OR

This activity, too, encourages reasoning about number size.

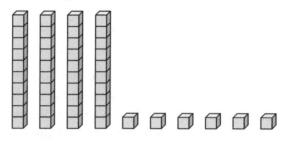

Play with a friend, but DO NOT look at what each other rolls.

Each of you:

   • Rolls a die to tell how many 10 rods you get.

   • Rolls again to tell how any 1s you get.

You want to have the GREATEST amount.

Decide whether to keep or switch the amount of 10s and 1s you have.

The person with the greatest number wins.

> Students benefit from additional practice in adding 10. You might play this circle game with the class. It is fun mostly because it's a game, but it also provides lots of math practice.

It is probably best to start with a number like 12, 13, 14, . . . , and so forth. It is not a good idea to start with a number with a 7 or even a number with 8 or 9 in it, but the starting number can vary widely. For example, if 10 children are in a circle and the teacher says 13 to start, Child 1 says 23, Child 2 says 33, Child 3 says 43, Child 4 says 53, and Child 5 says 63. Child 6 says 73 and is removed from the circle. After 83 and 93, the next child says 12.

Alternatively, you can start with a high number and change the rule to subtracting 10.

Your teacher says a number and writes it down so everyone will remember it.

When it is your turn, you say a number that is 10 more than the number the person before you said.

If you say a number with a 7 in it, you leave the circle.

If your number would be past 100, go back and say a number that is ONE LESS than the original number.

The last person left in the circle wins.

OR

To practice 10 more and 10 less, a student gives a clue about a number on the 100-chart. For example: *I am thinking of a number that is in the top half of the chart near the middle.* The student then calls on someone who must say the number that is 10 less. If she or he is correct, that person gives the next clue. If not, the original student calls on someone else.

I am thinking of a number on the 100-chart.

I will give you a clue about where my number is located.

My clue: _____

What number is 10 less than my number?

0	1	2	3	4	5	6	7	8	9
10	11	12	13	14	15	16	17	18	19
20	21	22	23	24	25	26	27	28	29
30	31	32	33	34	35	36	37	38	39
40	41	42	43	44	45	46	47	48	49
50	51	52	53	54	55	56	57	58	59
60	61	62	63	64	65	66	67	68	69
70	71	72	73	74	75	76	77	78	79
80	81	82	83	84	85	86	87	88	89
90	91	92	93	94	95	96	97	98	99

[*Possible clue:* I am thinking of a number that is in the top left of the chart and close to the edge. It is less than 40.]

➤ Students need to develop facility in estimating quantities when provided a referent quantity. They might engage in tasks like these:

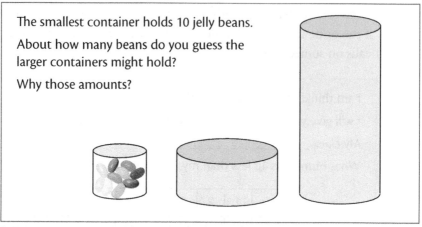

The smallest container holds 10 jelly beans.

About how many beans do you guess the larger containers might hold?

Why those amounts?

[*Likely estimates:* 35, 90.]

OR

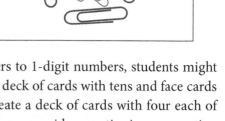

Grab a handful of paper clips.

Look at them.

Estimate how many there are.

Check by counting.

➤ To build facility with adding 2-digit numbers to 1-digit numbers, students might play a game like this. They can use a regular deck of cards with tens and face cards removed; aces count as 1. Or you might create a deck of cards with four each of the numbers 1–9 written on one side. The game provides practice in representing amounts, but primarily in adding and comparing.

Play with a partner.

Turn over 2 cards from a deck of cards to make a 2-digit number.

Turn over a third card to add to your number.

The greatest total wins a point.

Repeat the steps.

You win the game with 10 points.

OR

This game provides practice with subtraction involving 2-digit numbers and 1-digit numbers. Students use decks of cards as described for the activity above.

Choose 2 cards from a deck of cards to make a 2-digit number.

Then make up numbers to fill in the blanks so the total is your number.

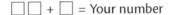 + = Your number

OR

The game below provides practice with adding 1-digit numbers or 10 to 2-digit numbers while it also benefits from randomness, which makes it reusable. This time, the random choices come from the children themselves.

Two players play.

The first player says any 2-digit number she or he wishes below 20.

The other player holds out any number of fingers she or he wishes and adds that number to the original number. This is the new total.

Take turns holding out fingers, each time adding to the earlier total.

The first person whose total gets above 75 wins.

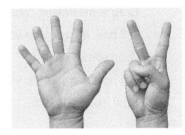

➤ To practice adding multiples of 10 to 2-digit numbers and subtracting multiples of 10, students might use the menu shown on the next page. Ordering food is always fun. Even a single use of this task involves a couple of additions and a subtraction. Reuse allows for more possibilities.

Choose an item from the food list.

Then choose a drink.

Tell how much your lunch would cost for the food and the drink.

Now change your drink.

What would the price be now?

How much more or less does one drink cost than the other?

Food		Drinks	
Burger	75¢	Milk	30¢
Sandwich	55¢	Juice	40¢
Taco	49¢	Pop	20¢
Noodles	39¢		

OR

The activity here practices subtraction of multiples of 10. Since kids love to drop things, they should be eager to do multiple subtractions.

Grab some linking cube trains (10 cubes long).

Tell how many cubes you have.

Drop some trains.

Tell how many cubes you dropped.

How many cubes are left?

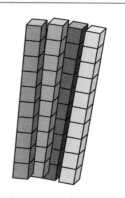

Suggestions for Home Activities: 1st Grade

Let parents know about the math their children are working on. You might provide short postings on a blog or short videos on your school website or elsewhere online to make the math ideas clear to the parents so they can support their children.

In particular, emphasize the difference between strategies and procedures, and share strategies your students are using for addition and subtraction and not just procedures. Encourage parents to stress employing strategies as their children approach novel situations and not simply application of procedures.

➤ Encourage parents to find opportunities to read 2-digit numbers to their children and have the children read those numbers to them. It might be addresses, prices, or numbers in the media.

➤ Share some of the games described in the preceding activities so that parents can play them with their children at home as well. You might prepare baggies with other games and the necessary materials in them or just describe the games to parents so that they can play them with their children.

The games could support place value work with numbers under 100 or addition of 2-digit and 1-digit numbers, addition or subtraction of 10, addition of 2-digit numbers and multiples of 10, or subtraction of multiples of 10. Two examples of such games are provided below. Another source of games is *Shuffling into Math with Fun Family Games* (Box Cars and One-Eyed Jacks, 2015).

Concentration

Prepare 24 cards, half of which show 2-digit numbers and half of which show what those numbers would look like using linking cube trains. Each number card should have a corresponding cube card. For example, here would be two matching cards:

 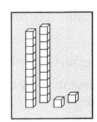

One, two, or more players can play.

Shuffle the cards and lay out 4 rows of 6 cards each.

Play "concentration" by turning over 2 cards at a time.

If they match (number and cubes), you keep them. If not, you turn them back over.

The player with the most kept cards wins the game.

Adding

Two players play.

Each rolls two dice to get a 2-digit number.

Then the player keeps rolling one die to get a number to add and keeps a running total.

The first person who hits 80 wins the game.

2nd Grade

These activities provide engaging learning and practice opportunities.

➤ To help students learn the names for the multiples of 100, you might provide this opportunity. Provide cards labeled 1, 2, 3, . . . , 9, turned over, so that students cannot see them.

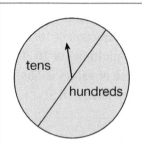

Choose a card to tell you how many tens or hundreds you will describe.

Then spin the spinner to say whether it will be tens or hundreds.

Write the number you created.

Say the name of your number.

➤ To provide practice skip counting by 5s, 10s, and 100s, you might set up a group of students, whether the whole class or a smaller group, in a circle. You start things off, probably using a low 2-digit number. Students follow the rules described below. You can vary the game skip counting by 10s or 100s.

Your teacher says a number to start.

When it's your turn, say the number that's 5 more than what the last person said.

If you end up saying a number with a 4 in it, pull out of the circle.

The last person left wins.

➤ Students need to see that numbers that have lots of hundreds, as compared to lots of tens or ones, are generally greater. That requires you to ask them, after the activity shown on the next page, what they noticed about the numbers that are worth the most.

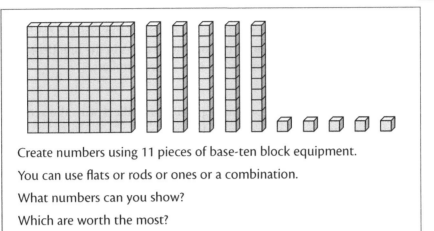

Create numbers using 11 pieces of base-ten block equipment.

You can use flats or rods or ones or a combination.

What numbers can you show?

Which are worth the most?

[*Possible values to use:* 11, 56, 110, 155, 416, 911, and so forth.]

> Students might enjoy puzzles like the ones below. The rules can be changed so that the activity can be reused; for example, an alternate rule might be that the tens digit is more than the hundreds digit but less than the ones digit. In each case students are practicing representations of 2-digit or 3-digit numbers.

For each of these rules, write 3 numbers that meet the rule and 3 numbers that do not:

- A 2-digit number where the tens digit is greater than the ones digit

- A 2-digit number that you can represent with 3 more base-ten ones cubes than base-ten tens rods

- A 3-digit number where the hundreds digit is 2 more than the ones digit

- A 3-digit number that you can represent with 2 more base-ten tens rods than base-ten ones cubes

[*Possible solutions that meet the requirements of each of the four rules, in sequence:* 52; 58 or 91 (8 tens and 11 ones); 230; 486.]

> Students might enjoy making up riddles about 2-digit or 3-digit numbers based on place value ideas. You might share a sample riddle first. For example:

I have a digit of 3 and two other digits.
I am more than 900.
I have one digit that is 3 more than another one.
What number could I be?

[*Possible solution:* 936.]

Make up riddles so someone can guess the number you are thinking of.

Make sure your clues are about either digits in the number or whether your number is more or less than other numbers.

> Students can practice representing 3-digit numbers with the activity below. Provide a bin full of base-ten flats, rods, and ones.

Dip both hands into the bin and pull out some blocks.

Tell the value of what you pulled out and write that number correctly.

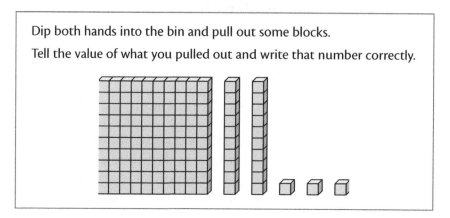

> Students should realize that 2-digit and 3-digit numbers can be represented in many ways. A task like the one below encourages that sort of thinking. You might notice (although students may or may not) something special about how a number like 21 can be represented—with 21 blocks (21 ones) or 12 blocks (1 one and 11 ones) or 3 blocks (2 tens and 1 one)—every time a trade is made to reduce the number of blocks, 9 fewer blocks are used.

A number can be represented correctly with 21 base-ten blocks or 3 base-ten blocks. What might that number be?

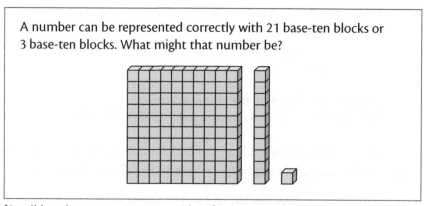

[*Possible values:* 300, 201, 111, and so forth. For example, 300 can be represented as 3 flats or as 1 flat + 20 rods; 111 can be represented as 1 flat + 1 rod + 1 one or as 10 tens + 11 ones.]

> ➤ To provide practice adding several 2-digit numbers at a time, you might ask students to work out these computations.

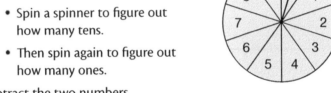

You must use the digits 1–9, each once, to fill in the blanks to make all of these equations true:

$23 + 45 + \Box\Box = 10\Box$ $8\Box + 2\Box + 1\Box = 13\Box$

$\Box 4 + 3\Box = 62$

[*Solution:* 23 + 45 + 36 = 104; 89 + 27 + 15 = 131; 24 + 38 = 62.]

> ➤ Students might play the game below to practice subtracting 2-digit numbers. The choice of how to award points is random; alternative rules could be created.

Two players play.

Each player does this twice:

- Spin a spinner to figure out how many tens.
- Then spin again to figure out how many ones.

Subtract the two numbers.

The player with an answer closest to 30 gets a point.

The first player with 10 points wins the game.

OR

The activity below provides an opportunity for students to learn about some real-life measurements that involve 2-digit and 3-digit numbers. Some computation is involved in the comparison of weights.

A big St. Bernard dog and a small poodle are on the same elevator.

About how many pounds do you think each might weigh?

About how much heavier do you think the big dog is?

[*Possible weights:* 175 pounds and 13 pounds.]

> The next several activities provide practice using concrete materials to add or subtract 3-digit numbers. In the first activity below, having students use their phone numbers is personal to them and they will enjoy that. There is straightforward practice in figuring out the difference, but deciding whether there are usually 2-digit or 3-digit answers cultivates reasoning. Normally, when we subtract 3-digit numbers, there are 3-digit answers; there are only 2-digit answers when the numbers are less than 100 apart.

Write the number that is the last 3 digits of your phone number.

Now write the number that is the first 3 digits.

Subtract the smaller number from the greater one, using base-ten blocks to help you.

Do most students in the class get 2-digit answers or 3-digit answers?

OR

The attractiveness of this game is the use of the spinner and the associated randomness. The game provides practice in addition and comparison. Rules could be changed to provide subtraction practice.

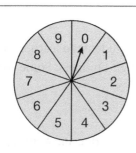

Play with a partner.

Spin the spinner 3 times to make a 3-digit number.

Take 3 more spins to make another 3-digit number.

Figure out the total of your numbers.

The player with the greatest total gets a point.

The first player with 10 points wins the game.

OR

This particular activity is "magic." Notice that if you add 418 and 107, and then subtract 25, you get 500, so subtracting 500 "magically" gets you back to the starting number. You could create other tricks by changing the added and subtracted numbers.

Try this trick.

One person chooses a 3-digit number but does not tell you what it is.

That person should add 418, subtract 25, and then add 107.

He or she then tells you the answer.

You have to surprise him by figuring out his or her starting number (and you can).

OR

The activity below involves some real-life contexts for math. The focus is on subtraction in terms of comparison. Giving choice both empowers children and provides extra problems at the same time.

You want to buy a computer or a tablet.

How much more might you have to spend for the computer than the tablet?

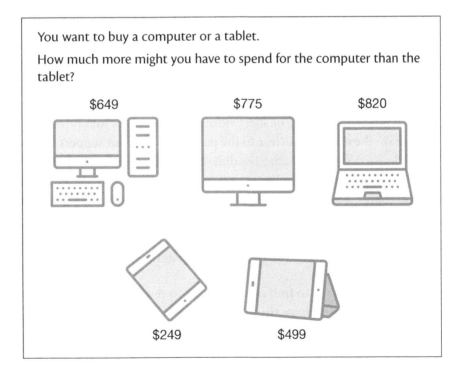

$649 $775 $820

$249 $499

OR

In this case, the practice involves regrouping and thinking of subtraction as adding up.

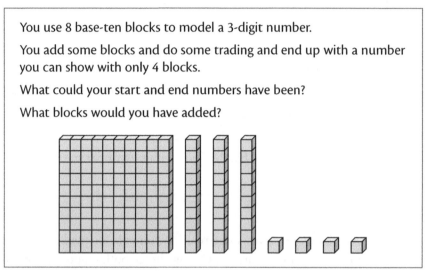

You use 8 base-ten blocks to model a 3-digit number.

You add some blocks and do some trading and end up with a number you can show with only 4 blocks.

What could your start and end numbers have been?

What blocks would you have added?

[*Possible solutions:* Start with 134 (1 flat, 3 rods, and 4 ones) and end with 301 (3 flats and 1 one) by adding 167, or start with 206 and end with 220 by adding 14.]

Suggestions for Home Activities: 2nd Grade

Let parents know about the math their children are working on. You might provide short postings on a blog or short videos on your school website or elsewhere online to make the math ideas clear to the parents so they can support their children.

In particular, emphasize the difference between strategies and procedures, and share strategies your students are using for addition and subtraction and not just procedures. Encourage parents to stress employing strategies as their children approach novel situations and not simply application of procedures.

Also show parents websites where they can access base-ten manipulatives for students to use for any 3-digit addition or subtraction they model for their parents.

➤ Encourage parents to find opportunities to read 2-digit and 3-digit numbers to their children and have the children read those numbers to them. It might be addresses, prices, or numbers in the media.

➤ Share some of the games described in the preceding activities so that parents can play them with their children at home as well. You might prepare baggies with other games and the necessary materials in them or just describe the games to parents so that they can play them with their children.

The games could support place value work with numbers under 1000 or addition and subtraction of 2-digit and 3-digit numbers. Here are two examples:

Concentration

Prepare 24 cards, half of which show an addition or subtraction involving mostly 2-digit numbers and half of which have the answer to one of the operations. Each operation card should have a corresponding answer card. For example, these would be two matching cards:

| 85 | 100 – 15 |

One, two, or more players can play.

Shuffle the cards and lay out 4 rows of 6 cards each.

Play "concentration" by turning over 2 cards at a time.

If the cards match (operation and answer), you keep them. If not, you turn them back over.

The player with the most kept cards wins the game.

Adding

Two players play.

Each rolls three dice to get a 3-digit number.

Then the player keeps rolling two dice to get a 2-digit number to add and keeps a running total.

The first person who hits 600 wins the game.

❖ CHAPTER 5 ❖

Measurement and Data

THIS CHAPTER focuses separately on both measurement and data concepts young students encounter.

THE FUNDAMENTALS

What Is Measurement?

Children are often interested in which item is bigger and which is smaller; this suggests that measurement matters to them. But what is measurement? Essentially, measurement is a system that allows us to quantify how much or how little of some **attribute** an object possesses. When we work with **units**, we are essentially comparing how much of that attribute an object possesses with how much the unit possesses; even without units, we can find ways to compare how much of an attribute one object possesses relative to another.

For example, we might say that one child is taller than another because we know how many inches tall each one is and we can compare those numbers. But we might also compare the children directly by standing them beside each other and see that, even without using numbers, one has more height than another since one height is all of the second height and some more; the comparison is still based on quantification.

Important Measurement Principles

A few common principles apply to any measurement, whatever it is. These include the following:

Different measures of an object might be unrelated. For example, an item might have lots of weight but not much height.

Students should have opportunities to see that an object can often be measured and compared with another object in many ways.

What are some things you could measure about these thermoses that would let you compare them?

[*Possible solutions:* How tall they are, how much they hold, how wide they are.]

You might also want to engage children in class discussion so that they can see that different children consider different attributes when deciding what is big and what is little.

Describe some things you think are big.

What makes them big?

Describe some things you think are little.

What makes them little?

Sometimes it is possible to measure directly, but sometimes not. For example, to decide whether one object is longer than another when they cannot be brought together, you might use units, which is an indirect measurement, or you might compare each to a third object that is transportable, such as a piece of string.

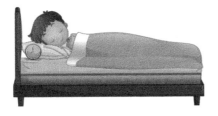

It is useful to know some measurements to help you figure out others. For example, if you know how long your arm is, it might help you measure a desk, as shown on the next page.

When you use units, you must repeatedly use the same unit (or many copies of the same unit) without leaving gaps or creating overlaps in the case of length or area. For example, you cannot measure an area with some big squares and some small ones and then count all the squares to quantify the area. To just say the area below is 21 squares would be misleading.

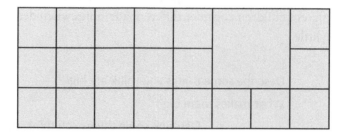

If you change the unit, you are likely to have to change how many of that unit describe the measure of an item. For example, if you measure a large pitcher in baby cups, you will get a different value for its size than if you measure it in large cups. Or if you measure a length in inches, you will get a different answer than if you measure it in feet.

It is not possible to be exact when measuring a continuous attribute such as length, area, or capacity. Any measurement that does not involve counting discrete objects is a **continuous** measurement, because it can hold any value (even a fractional value). For example, even if we say that something is exactly 3 cm, it really isn't. It might be a minuscule amount more or less.

Stages of Measurement Instruction

No matter what measurement we might talk about, there are generally three stages of instruction that make sense for that measurement, even if they are not all dealt with in the primary years. The stages are described below.

Stage 1: Definition/Comparison. It is at this stage when students learn what the measurement is all about and learn the technique one would use to decide which object has more of that measure.

For example, measurement of length is about lining two objects against each other with a common start position, and if one extends beyond the other, it has more length. Measuring weight is about putting two objects on opposite sides of a **pan balance** and determining which side hangs down farther.

Stage 2: Nonstandard Units. It is at this stage when students begin to use everyday objects repeatedly, one after the other (**iterating**), to determine how many units long or wide the object is or how much space it occupies.

For example, measuring the length of an object might involve lining up toothpicks, leaving no gaps, and figuring out how many toothpicks it would take to extend the full length of the item. A measurement of capacity might require determining how many cups you would have to fill in order to empty a larger container.

Stage 3: Standard Units. It is at this stage when students begin to use agreed-upon conventional units to quantify a particular attribute of an object.

For example, length might be measured in inches or feet. Weight might be measured in pounds or kilograms.

There are those who believe that the nonstandard unit phase is unnecessary, but many believe that it is useful for two reasons. One is that it helps clarify what the attribute is, differentiating it from the tool used (e.g., *Length does not mean inches. Length is not about using a ruler.*) (Godfrey & O'Connor, 1995). When a child uses a ruler and just reads a number of 10 or 12 off the scale, it doesn't really clarify that there were 12 units, each 1 inch long, that were iterated to fit that length. Another benefit of focusing on nonstandard units is that in everyday life, we often use handy, but nonstandard, units.

Length

Length is an attribute that is **1-dimensional**. It describes extent. Lots of vocabulary is associated with length, including terms such as height, distance, width, and so forth.

> ### Comparing and Ordering Lengths Without Units

Generally, students compare lengths directly, putting one object against the other at the same starting point, before they compare indirectly (Szilagyi, Clements, & Sarama, 2013).

Direct Comparison. It is critical that children realize that there must be a common starting point when two lengths are directly compared. Otherwise, the results might be misleading.

The dark arrow below is longer, but it might not look that way if the ends are not lined up.

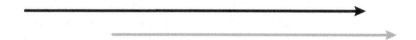

Students also need to learn that the length must be "straightened out," so that, again, there would be nothing misleading. The curly line below does not look longer than the straight one, but it is.

It is important for students to show a teacher that they really know how to test whether one item is longer than another. On a table, you might place a variety of long, thin items, such as a straw, a playdough snake, a pencil, a stapler, a child's belt, and a necktie. Then students might be given the task shown at the top of the next page:

> Choose something on the table.
>
> Find 5 items around the room that are longer than your item and 5 that are shorter than it.
>
> Find 3 items that are really close to the same length as your item.

Indirect Comparison. Sometimes, a person might want to compare two lengths/ heights/distances when the two objects cannot be brought next to each other. The objects might be, for example, a window in one room and a window in another. Eventually, students will learn to use units to do the comparison, but before that they might use a third transportable object to help.

If a student uses a piece of string and cuts it to the length of one window, he or she could take that string over to the other window to see if it extends beyond the length associated with the first window or not. This kind of comparison only makes sense, though, if students recognize **conservation of length**, that is, if they realize that the length of the string cannot change just because it was moved.

The activity below might be useful in providing a chance for students to use indirect measurement.

> Here is a ball of yarn.
>
> How could it help you figure out whether the bookshelf at the side of the room is longer than the bookshelf in the front or not?

➤ *Using Nonstandard Units*

A unit of length is an essentially 1-dimensional item that is copied or partitioned and compared with other lengths. For example, a unit of length could be a foot (represented by a ruler block) or a pencil:

Both of those items are actually **3-dimensional**, not 1-dimensional, but only one dimension is considered when the item is used as the unit. It is always best if the unit used really accentuates the one attribute it is being used to measure. For length, that would mean items that are essentially long and skinny.

Nonstandard units, often called unconventional units, are units that are not part of the **Imperial** or **metric system**. The units might be toothpicks, pencils, straws, paperclips, and so forth. Sometimes students might use parts of their body, since the unit will always be available. It might be the width of a finger, the width of a hand, the length of a foot, etc.

By using units, whether standard or nonstandard, students can compare the lengths of objects indirectly, using the numbers of units instead of the items themselves.

Measuring. To measure with a nonstandard length unit, a student must iterate that unit without leaving any gaps and keeping the units in a straight line. It is easier for students when they have many identical copies of the unit.

For example, a student might line up a set of identical new pencils (not used, so they are identical) along a desk to measure how many pencils long the desk is. Sometimes the student must use a partial unit if the item is not an exact number of units. Students can learn to either estimate a fraction (in later grades) or just say "a little more than x units" or "between x and y units."

Sometimes it is inconvenient or impossible to use many copies of the same unit. In this case, a student might use one unit over and over. When this is required, it is particularly important to keep track of where one copy of the unit ends and the next copy begins. This is often difficult for children, so estimates need to be accepted. For example, a student might measure the length of the sandbox by using his or her foot over and over along the edge of the sandbox.

Many students, whether because of a lack of understanding of what is meant by a measurement or because they lack appropriate motor skill precision, have difficulty ensuring that they appropriately line up units without gaps or overlaps to measure length. It is important to observe their skills in this regard before assigning them too many tasks that require measuring with units.

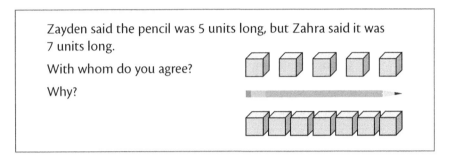

Zayden said the pencil was 5 units long, but Zahra said it was 7 units long.

With whom do you agree?

Why?

Occasionally, two copies of a unit can be used so the two can be lined up. Then the first one is moved after the next one is in place.

Now move the first pencil:

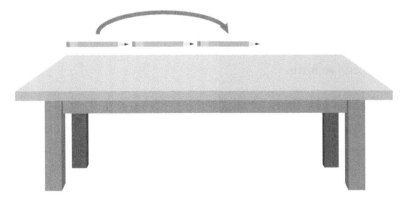

Comparing and Ordering by Length. Students learn that to compare the sizes of two objects that have been measured in the same unit, the number of units is all that matters; the items need not be available. That, of course, is one of the reasons we use units, whether standard on nonstandard.

Students need opportunities to see that measurements vary depending on the unit used. You might have children lie down on a long sheet of paper and have a peer trace around them or draw a line to show their height. You can also provide a number of possible units, such as straws, erasers, crayons, Cuisenaire rods of different colors, toothpicks, or paper clips.

> Choose 5 different "units" to use to measure how tall you are.
>
> Predict which number of units will be greatest.
>
> See if you are right.

Students also need to learn that the same unit must be used consistently for the comparison to be meaningful. For example, one item might be 3 paper clips long and another 4. So it seems like the second item is longer. But if the 3 paper clips were long ones and the 4 paper clips were short ones, that assumption may or may not be correct.

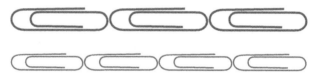

Sometimes it is useful to compare the lengths of more than two items. In this case, ordering the lengths of a lot of items requires a lot of comparisons. Students need to be systematic:

- Compare two items.
- Take a third item and decide if it is shorter than both, longer than both, or between them.
- Take the next item and compare it to each of the already ordered items, and so forth.

> Using Standard Units

Why We Use Standard Units. We use standard units primarily for better communication. If you are on the phone and tell someone that something is 17 inches long, they know exactly what you mean. If you had said that it was 3 pencils long, they would have to wonder about what sort of pencil you were using. It is also practical to use standard units because lots of tools for measuring are readily available, such as 12-inch rulers, meter sticks, yardsticks, and so forth.

Standard Units We Use. In most countries, the metric system is used, and the main units for primary students are centimeters and meters. In the United States, students meet these units as well as inches, feet, and yards. Clearly, centimeters and inches are used to measure smaller items, although they can be used for longer items as well. Meters, yards, and feet are normally used for longer items.

It is useful for students to learn the abbreviations for the units too:

Inches	" *or* in.
Feet	ft.
Yards	yd.
Centimeters	cm
Meters	m

Typical structured items that come in centimeter lengths are base-ten blocks and Cuisenaire rods. Structured items that commonly come in inches include wooden blocks that are 1" cubes or square tiles, which are often 2" on a side.

Students in 2nd grade learn about formal length units that include inches, feet, centimeters, and meters. They might also learn about yards. It is important that they develop benchmarks for each of these units as well as having a sense of the relationship between them. So you might ask:

> What part of you is about an inch?
>
> What part of you is about a centimeter?
>
> What everyday item is about a foot long?
>
> What everyday item is about a meter long?

[*Possible solutions:* One of the 3 sections of my middle finger, the length of a nail, a ruler, a window's height, respectively.]

Effect of Unit Size. Students could explore the effect of unit size with nonstandard units, but the Common Core curriculum (2010) calls for students to explore the effect of unit size with standard units. Essentially, students need to learn that it takes more small units (whether standard or nonstandard) to measure a length than it would take larger units; or, in other words, it takes fewer large units (like meters or yards) to measure a distance or length than small units (like inches or feet).

This concept is very important in number as well as in measurement. When we skip count by 5s, it takes longer to get to a number than if we skip count by 10s. This is because it takes more smaller units to describe an amount than larger units.

Using a Ruler/Yardstick/Meter Stick. There are a lot of issues to consider for students learning to use a ruler. Probably the most important is for them to understand where the numbers on the ruler come from and what they represent.

Ideally, the first time a child uses a ruler, she or he lines up inch or centimeter units (depending on which ruler is used) along the edge of the ruler to see that 2 appears on the ruler where 2 units end, 3 appears where 3 units end, and so forth. This gives meaning to the numbers; something is 2" long when it goes from 0 to 2 on the ruler, since two of those 1" units would fit there. Students might use 1" wooden cubes for an inch ruler or unit base-ten blocks for a centimeter ruler.

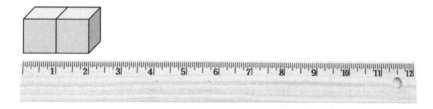

Similarly, it is valuable for students to see that 12 inches make a foot by lining up 12 unit cubes along a 12" ruler, that 3 feet make a yard by lining up three rulers along a yardstick, and that 100 centimeters make 1 meter by lining up 100 small cubes (or 10 base-ten rods that are each 10 cm long) along a meter stick.

Students need to understand that we start at the edge of the ruler (sometimes labeled 0 and sometimes not) or at the first mark at the edge of the ruler (in case there is a little extra space to allow for wear) to be able to just say the number at the other end of the item as the measured value. For example, this paper clip is 3 cm long.

However, it is not necessary to start at 0. The item can start anywhere, so long as the difference between the end reading and the start reading is calculated. The paper clip is still 3 cm long even if it is measured as shown below, since 5 − 2 = 3.

So students should realize that we start at 0 for convenience, to avoid a calculation, not because it is required.

For some items, particularly curved items, flexible measuring tapes are obviously advantageous as compared to rulers, yardsticks, or meter sticks.

➤ *Estimating Using Benchmarks*

When students establish some benchmarks for the units they use or other benchmarks, it helps them to estimate lengths. Useful benchmarks might be:

- A ruler is 1 foot or 12 inches. So is a football.
- The width of a finger is about 1 centimeter.
- A hand span is about 4 inches or 10 centimeters.
- A door is about 2 meters high.
- A yard is about the length of a baseball bat.
- A small paper clip is about 3 centimeters.
- A pencil or a hot dog is about 6 inches.

To estimate, students might relate the amount to be measured to one of these benchmarks. An activity like this one will give them practice:

Find something in the room that you think is each length.

Then check your predictions.

- About 2 feet   • About 50 centimeters
- About 15 inches   • About 2 meters

➤ *Solving Measurement Problems*

There are many situations where we might want to add or compare measurements, particularly measurements in the same units. For example, someone might have measured two pieces of baseboard material and want to know how much more they need to finish the baseboard in the room. Or someone might want to know exactly how many inches taller one child is than another. All of these types of problems provide contexts in which number skills and concepts can be practiced.

One valuable tool to use to solve these problems is the open number line. For example, suppose you had measured two bookshelves; one was 28 inches long and the other was 36 inches long. You want to know how much longer the longer shelf is. A number line can help you solve the problem: $36 - 28 = \square$.

Area, Capacity, and Weight

In the primary grades, the Common Core curriculum (2010) introduces measurement of attributes such as area, capacity, and weight. In Pre-K through Grade 2, students remain in Stage 1 of measurement instruction—definition/comparison—and do not progress to the use of standard or even nonstandard units for measures of these three properties.

> ### Comparing Areas

Area is defined as the **2-dimensional** amount of space that something takes up. One might be interested in the area of a geometric shape such as a rectangle or triangle, or the area of interest could be the base of a 3-dimensional object like a placemat, a bedsheet, a piece of loose-leaf paper, or a sticky note.

To decide if one area is greater than another, a student can superimpose one shape on the other to see if there is any space left over. For example, the gray shape below is smaller than the white one since it fits on top and there is space left. The gray area is less than the white area.

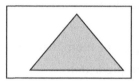

Sometimes, a shape may need to be cut and rearranged to determine whether it fits on top of another shape or not. Part of the gray shape below extends beyond the white rectangle, so the excess needs to be cut and moved to see whether or not it uses up all of the rest of the white space.

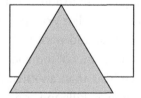 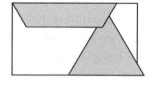

It is pretty clear that the little bit of gray overhang would not come close to filling the available white space, so the gray shape is smaller in area than the white shape.

Directly comparing areas can be easy for students when one item is very obviously smaller in area than another, but when they are close, it is trickier. Students need to think about decomposing one shape and rearranging it to reach a decision. To help students develop this approach, you might ask questions like the ones shown on the next page.

Which of these pieces of paper do you think is bigger?

How sure are you?

How can you check?

➤ *Comparing Capacity*

Capacity describes how much a container can hold. People measure capacities of a variety of things, typically drinking glasses, pitchers, vases, drawers, closets, and so on. Students in the primary grades look only at capacity comparison and do not use units.

Because capacities involve 3-dimensional items, superposition is not possible. And if units are not used, the only way to really compare capacity is to fill one item with a pourable material (e.g., water, flour, sugar, rice, or sand) and pour the contents into another container.

Either the contents of the first container exactly fill the other container and the capacities are equal, or the contents do not fill the other container, in which case the capacity of the first item is less, or there is still material left even after filling the second container and the capacity of the first container is greater.

To ensure that students know how to directly compare two containers to decide which holds more, you might set up a task where you have two containers that are not identical that you know hold the same amount and one that holds less, but not a whole lot less. Then you might present the task below.

Which of these containers hold the same amount?

Which does not?

> *Comparing Weight*

Weight describes how heavy something is. Weight is a tough attribute for students to work with since there are no visual cues unless the student happens to be familiar with items made of the particular material used for the item in question.

Often small things,
in terms of **volume**,
are very heavy.

Often big things
are not very heavy.

The only way, without units, for a student to test which item is heavier is to use a pan balance to see which side goes down.

Students might just hold both items, one in each hand, and use their own bodies like pan balances. They will probably be able to tell which item is heavier if the difference between the weights is enough, but not if the weights are close.

Time

The work on time in the curriculum for young students is focused more on reading clocks and telling time than it is on measuring time. However, time is a measurable attribute, and a teacher might talk about how to determine whether one event takes more time than another when comparing measurements. This might be accomplished by starting both events at the same time and seeing which continues when the other is over; this is much like length comparison.

➤ *Reading a Clock*

Although most of the clocks in our lives now are digital, the curriculum requires that students learn to read **analog clocks** (i.e., those with faces and hands) as well as digital clocks.

Initially, students learn to read times to the nearest hour. On an analog clock, the student must be told that, on the hour, the long hand (the minute hand) points to the top, or 12, and the hour is the number to which the small hand (the hour hand) is pointing. On a digital clock, the hour is followed by a colon and two zeroes.

8 o'clock

At some point, students begin to tell times to the half-hour or to the nearest 5 minutes. It is useful for students to begin with a clock with moving hands, especially one that marks the minute numbers around the clock.

Students learn that every time the number under the minute hand changes, 5 more minutes have passed, so the ability to count by 5s is very handy for telling time.

When students initially learn to read hour and half-hour times on a clock, they need to be taught the conventions of what the two hands represent. They also need to learn the difference between a.m. and p.m. and whether a clock shows that difference. Notice that the suggested question at the top of the next page does not indicate whether the clock is digital or analog, so students are free to choose whichever they wish, or both.

> Think about what a clock looks like at seven o'clock in the morning and eight thirty at night.
>
> How do the times look different?

You might even suggest an activity like the one below:

> The two hands of a clock are fairly close together.
>
> What time might it be? Write the time in digital format.

You may choose to introduce the terms "quarter after" or "quarter to" as alternate ways to read times like 8:15 or 8:45.

➤ Writing Times

Students need to learn to write times digitally (e.g., 35 minutes after 8 as 8:35 or 50 minutes after 9 as 9:50). Inevitably students will learn that there are 60 minutes in an hour, and 5 minutes after 9:55 comes 10:00.

➤ a.m. and p.m.

Students should learn the difference between times that are written as a.m. and those that are written as p.m. It is probably not wise to suggest that a.m. is in the morning and p.m. is in the afternoon since there are a.m. times in the middle of the night and p.m. times also during the night.

But students can learn that during the school day, the morning is a.m. and the afternoon is p.m. They can also learn that we switch between a.m. and p.m. at 12 o'clocks.

Money

➤ Units We Use

Money is often thought of as a number topic, and in some ways it is. But at the same time, money value is a measurable attribute with units like cents and dollars. Nickels, dimes, and quarters are also money units. Just like centimeters are used for small lengths and meters for longer lengths, pennies (or cents), nickels, and dimes are used for small amounts of money, and quarters and dollars are used for somewhat larger amounts of money. Interestingly, we do not have units bigger than dollars. Students need to learn to use the symbol $ as an abbreviation for dollars and the symbol ¢ as an abbreviation for cents. There are no abbreviations for nickels, dimes, or quarters.

> *Solving Money Problems*

Money problems involve lots of numbers, whether the task is finding a total price, counting a set of coins, determining change, or finding out how much more one thing is worth than another. Students should have opportunities to solve these kinds of problems, at an appropriate difficulty level.

Data

Data has always been around, but in our society now, we are besieged by data. It is increasingly important that students gain an understanding of how data is used and interpreted.

> *Classifying and Sorting*

Data is often built on categorization or sorting. For example, we might compare primary children's and older children's reactions to something; that is a categorization of school children. We categorize academic subjects when we talk about disciplines: math, science, language, and so forth. We categorize people by the state in which they were born. Categories are everywhere.

Young children learn to categorize when they learned to say words like "chair," "boy," "house," and so forth, since they sort items in their environment into those that fit the category described by the word and those that do not.

So it is not surprising that curriculum standards regarding data exist for even our youngest children. Work in this area might start with asking students which of certain items belong in a particular category or another and perhaps having them tell both which and how many items fit in each category. For example, you might provide a number of pieces of fabric to students and ask them to put the red ones in one area and the purple ones in another. They might tell you how many they put in each category.

Children in the primary years sometimes take a group of items and sort or classify them by choosing their own categories. Other times, they are given a pre-sorted set of items and try to figure out the rule. For example, looking at the food items at the top of the next page, students might sort them in many ways:

- Ones I like and ones I do not like
- Ones that are green and ones that are not
- Ones that you cook and ones that you do not cook
- Ones that you keep in the fridge and ones that you do not keep in the fridge

Asking students to re-sort the same items in different ways is important. It helps them understand that one item can have a lot of "names." The notion of categorizing the same item using a different attribute comes up in number when a number might be called, in later grades, a whole number or a rational number, or even or a multiple of 4. It also comes up in geometry when a shape is sometimes called a square, but other times a rectangle or a polygon.

One of the strategies that a teacher can use to help a child think of ways to sort objects is to encourage him or her to think of many ways to describe one of the objects. An example is shown below, but many other examples are possible. In this case, students might think of soft, a toy, stuffed, and so forth.

What are some words you could use to describe this toy?

How might that help you if you were asked to sort some objects that included this toy?

Determining a possible **sorting rule** for a pre-sorted set is also important and requires a lot of reasoning. What is interesting is that sometimes two different people will come up with different rules, both of which make sense. For example, the items on the next page have been sorted into two groups, one group in each row. A good guess for the sorting rule might be that toys were put into Group 1 and the items that are not toys make up Group 2. But perhaps the first set of items are together because those are items that are stored in the basement of a house and the others are not. We can only speculate about a sorting rule; we can't be sure.

Group 1

Group 2

One of the tools students sometimes use is a sorting circle, or hoop. Items that fit the sorting rule are put in the hoop or circle and those that do not are left outside. This approach is a precursor to creation of a **Venn diagram**.

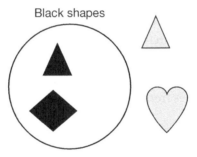

Some students will use two sorting rules at one time and, again, might use sorting hoops to help.

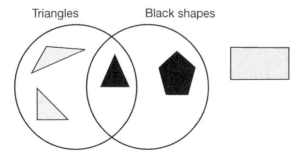

> ## *Reading and Interpreting Sorted Data*

Once items have been sorted, students should have opportunities to both describe what has happened and draw conclusions. For example, suppose a group of library books have been sorted as shown below:

Picture Books   Other Books

You might ask students to tell you how many books are or are not picture books; this question is about reading the data. But you might also ask them which type there are more of and how many more; this involves interpreting the data.

Sometimes interpreting the data might involve asking students why they think there might be more items in one category than another.

You might use an open task, such as the one below, to see whether students can draw inferences from a sort.

> You sorted a group of stuffed animals.
>
> There were 18 animals altogether, and there were 3 more teddy bears than pandas.
>
> Describe what all the categories might have been and how many animals might have been in each category.

> ## *Line Plots*

A **line plot** is a graph that shows how many items fit in different numerical categories. For example, a group of seven 1st-grade students might be compared in terms of how many are 6 years old and how many are 7 years old. The data could be shown in a line plot like the one on the next page.

Ages of 1st-Graders

```
X
X    X
X    X
X    X
_____
6    7    Years old
```

Normally, Xs are used in a line plot to show the items in a category. The categories are numerical and can be shown on a number line, as is the case here. It is easy to see on a line plot which category has the most items in it.

A line plot looks like what an adult would associate with a bar graph; the main difference is not so much about using the Xs, although that is different, but more about the requirement that the categories be numbers placed on a "number line." Like any graph, a line plot should have a title and labels to clarify what it is about.

One of the motivations for using a line plot is that it is pretty quick and easy to make Xs, requiring less effort than making squares or pictures, as would be the case for bar graphs or picture graphs.

Students can both read data off a line plot (e.g., how many are in a specific category) and make inferences (e.g., how many more are in one category than another, the total number of people represented in the plot, etc.).

In the Common Core curriculum (2010), line plots focus on measurements that are taken, to the nearest whole unit. A child might, for example, measure a variety of objects and indicate how many are various numbers of inches long.

You might suggest an activity like this one:

Jane measured the heights of 12 books on the bookshelf.

She made a line plot to show the results.

What does her plot tell you about the books she measured?

Numbers of Books

```
                      X
                      X
                 X    X
X          X    X    X
X          X    X    X
_____
6    7    8    9    10    Inches high
```

[*Possible solutions:* There are lots more tall books than short books. No books seem to be more than 10 inches high.]

➤ *Picture Graphs*

Picture graphs are graphs that represent how frequently various categories occur in a set of data by using pictures rather than the Xs used in line plots or the squares we use in bar graphs. The categories can be any categories, not necessarily numerical, as is required in line plots.

For example, this picture graph might be used to show how different numbers of students get to school:

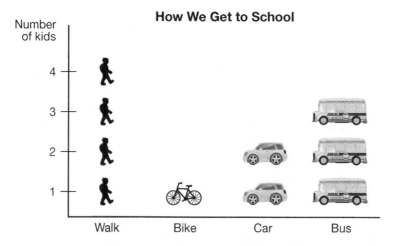

Notice that there are labels and titles, and the **scale** is also shown. The scale does not always have to be shown when the increment is 1, but it is a good idea to do so. Normally, the categories are placed apart from each other about the same distance.

Students need to learn that it is important that the pictures be similar in size, or the graph can be misleading. For example, it is clear from the graph above that more children walk than bike, travel by car, or take the bus. But the graph below does not make it so clear.

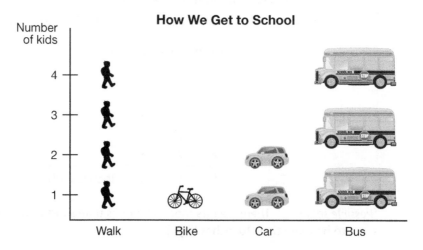

At this level, the scale for how many are in categories will always be a scale of 1; that changes for older students. Students might draw their own pictures, which need not be identical, but should be easy to interpret and the same overall size. Alternatively, students might use digital icons of some sort.

Students can not only read data off picture graphs but can draw conclusions as well. For example, the less misleading graph on the preceding page makes it clear that in this group of students, 1 more student walks than takes the bus and a total of 10 students provided information.

Many teachers precede work with picture graphs with work with concrete graphs. Rather than drawing or gluing on pictures of items, actual items are placed on the graph. For example, for the previous graph, the children themselves would be placed where the pictures are. Or the graph for the pattern block design (at the left below) can show how many of each type of block was used to create the design.

Blocks I Used

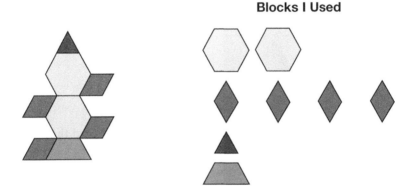

Egg cartons might be a useful way to create concrete graphs involving small objects to ensure that everything remains lined up.

➤ *Bar Graphs*

Bar graphs, much like picture graphs, show the numbers associated with different categories and allow quick and easy visual comparisons. Like picture graphs, bar graphs can be read or interpreted so long as titles and labels are provided. The only difference between the bar graph and the picture graph is that a square (or rectangle) is used to represent each item rather than a picture of the item. The squares can be kept separate (making the bar graph almost like a picture graph) but they are often connected to form a bar; this is why, of course, they are called bar graphs. Using squares or bars is a way to standardize items being tabulated and avoid misleading graphs.

Square tiles are an excellent tool for creating bar graphs. Students can line up the tiles (making a concrete graph) first and then convert their graph to picture form using gridded paper.

Horizontal or vertical bars can be used to represent the data. One axis shows the categories into which the information has been sorted and the other normally shows a frequency (i.e., how many items are in the category). Generally, the bars are equally wide, equally spaced, and not touching each other. Horizontal and vertical bar graph representations of data on kids' favorite pizza toppings are shown below:

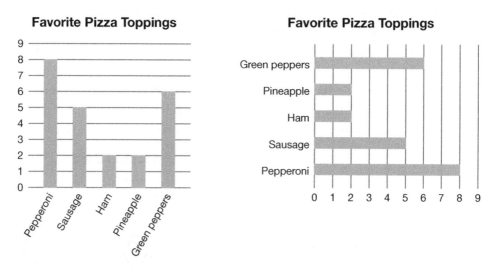

Graphs can be interpreted in a number of ways, and they make comparisons easy. For example, from either of the graphs above, a student could conclude that if the people who were asked were allowed to choose only one favorite topping, then 23 kids responded, more of them prefer pepperoni than anything else, and pineapple and ham are not very popular.

MISCONCEPTIONS TO WATCH FOR

➤ *Comparing Lengths Incorrectly When Part of a Length Is Hidden.* Sometimes when one length is partially blocked, a student does not take the part that is blocked into account. For example, a child might think that the thick line below is longer than the thin one since he or she is not including the part of the thin line behind the bowl.

> ***Comparing Lengths Incorrectly When Items Are Not Aligned.*** It is easy for a student to assume that the thin line below is longer since it extends further. The child forgets that the lines need to be lined up at one end to make a comparison.

> ***Comparing Lengths Incorrectly When One or More Lengths Are Not Straight.*** A child might think that the top line below is longer than the zigzag line since it sticks out farther.

The definition for length comparison requires that both items be extended to their full extent by being straightened out. Otherwise the length is not a fixed amount and would change depending on how you curve or zigzag the line. You might set up an activity like this one to emphasize this message for students:

Which of these strings do you think is longer?

Why? How can you be sure?

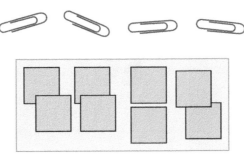

> ***Problems with Iteration.*** Some children struggle when laying out units to measure (whether for length or area) to ensure that there are no gaps or overlaps and, in the case of length, that the units form a line. This is partly a question of motor skills, but it does require monitoring on the part of the teacher and alerting students to the problem.

➤ *Reading Lengths Incorrectly Off a Ruler When Not Starting at 0.* If a child starts measuring at, for example, the 4 mark on a ruler and the item extends to the 9 mark, many children assume the length is 9 inches (or centimeters). They forget that they must remove the 4 units that were not included beside the item; there are really only 5 units of length for the item.

➤ *Incorrectly Relating Length to Area.* Some children assume that if an item is longer, it must have more area. For example, they might assume that the square below the rectangle here has less area because the rectangle is longer.

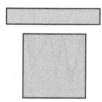

➤ *Incorrectly Relating Capacity to Height.* Some children assume that a container that is taller will hold more. Clearly that is not always the case, even though sometimes it is.

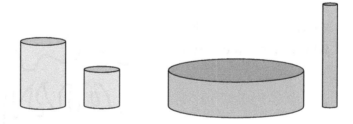

➤ *Incorrectly Relating Weight to Volume.* Some children assume that an item that has more volume must be heavier. For example, they might assume that a large plastic container is heavier than a small metal ball.

> *Confusing the Size of a Coin with Its Value.* For some children, it just does not make sense that a more valuable coin could be smaller. For that reason, they often underestimate the value of a dime or overestimate the value of a penny or nickel.

> *Ignoring Items When Sorting.* When students sort using a particular criterion, they sometimes have difficulty dealing with items that do not fit the sorting rule. For example, if there were a number of shapes and all of the squares were put together, they might have difficulty putting the shapes that differ into a single "other" pile. In their minds, the remaining shapes don't belong together since they are different from each other. So if the children were asked how many more squares there were than other shapes, they might say 3, since each of the items on the right in the example below is another shape for them; there is no group of 3 other shapes.

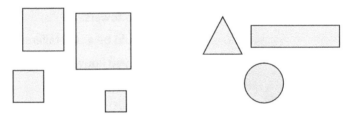

> *Misaligning Pictures on a Picture Graph or Line Plot.* If students use different-sized pictures on a picture graph or different-sized Xs on a line plot, then it could be hard to interpret quickly which category has the most or the fewest items.

How Long Were Our Pencils?

THE FUN

Pre-K and Kindergarten

These activities provide engaging learning and practice opportunities.

> It is fun to watch students try to figure out what is going on behind a screen. They need to realize that there is actually no way for them to know which string on the next page is longer since they don't know what is happening behind the screen.

> Which string do you think is longer? The thick one or the thin one?
>
> How sure are you?

> Students might enjoy building towers and comparing the towers' heights. Asking for a tower that is a LOT taller is more dramatic than just asking for one to be taller than another; students respond positively to this.

> Build two towers.
>
> One should be a LOT taller than the other.
>
> Tell how you know it is taller.

> Children always enjoying making patterns. They might choose to make a repeating pattern based on measurement, for example, a repeating long/short pattern or a repeating long/long/short pattern.

> Find some objects that you would call long and some you would call short.
>
> Make a repeating pattern that has a long item/short item repeat.

[*Possible solution:* Long Cuisenaire rod, short rod, short rod, long rod, short rod, short rod, and so forth.]

> Provide two toy cars and two identical ramps. Children might wonder which car will go farther when they go down the ramps. It would be interesting to watch how students react if the distances are close.

Start the cars down the ramps at the same time.

Predict which will go farther.

Does it?

> Students might engage in length comparisons in lots of other ways too. The activity below raises an interesting measurement hypothesis for students to explore. And the best part is that they get to run.

Stand next to a friend to decide who has longer legs.

Then both of you run as fast as you can across the room.

Do people with longer legs run faster?

OR

The activity below also is fun for students. It would be interesting to see if students independently figure out that they should start at the same starting place and fly the planes in the same direction.

You and a friend make paper airplanes.

Whose plane goes farther?

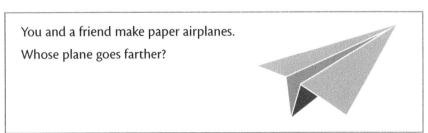

OR

Find a reference that has actual size animal footprints that can be copied so students can cut them out and compare them directly. Examples are *Track Pack: Animal Tracks in Full Life Size* (Gray, 2003) or *Actual Size* (Jenkins, 2011). This is much more interesting for students than comparing the areas of two random shapes.

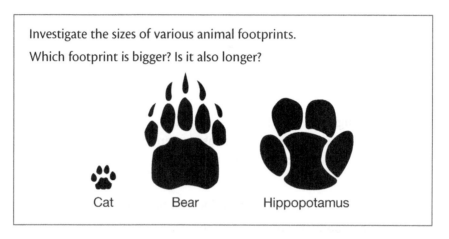

Investigate the sizes of various animal footprints.

Which footprint is bigger? Is it also longer?

Cat   Bear   Hippopotamus

> Students might compare areas in a variety of different situations. The activity below is valuable for its attention to important health information too.

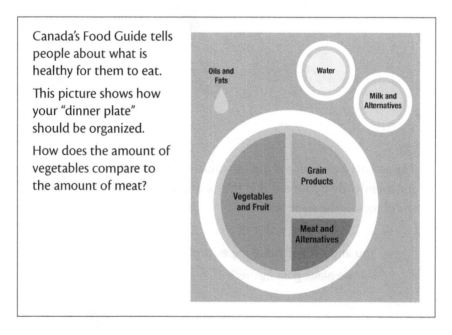

Canada's Food Guide tells people about what is healthy for them to eat.

This picture shows how your "dinner plate" should be organized.

How does the amount of vegetables compare to the amount of meat?

Oils and Fats

Water

Milk and Alternatives

Grain Products

Vegetables and Fruit

Meat and Alternatives

OR

Students will likely be curious as to whether taller trees always have bigger leaves. Or maybe wider trees have bigger leaves, or maybe leaf size is independent of the size of the tree. You might extend the activity below to encouraging students to learn about leaves from different parts of the world.

Collect leaves from different sorts of trees.

What kinds of trees have bigger leaves?

Which have smaller leaves?

OR

All children love mud puddles, but there is measurement associated with puddles too. You might choose a day after it has been raining and there are mud puddles around before suggesting this activity:

Go outdoors after a rainy day.

Choose two mud puddles you can see.

Which mud puddle do you think is bigger?

How can you check?

➤ One of the measurement attributes students might explore is capacity. There are a number of interesting activities for young children that involve volumes. Although we normally think of capacity in terms of liquids, our pockets also have capacity (as do drawers, cupboards, etc.).

Choose two items of clothing that have pockets.

Figure out a way to decide which pocket holds more.

OR

Asking students whether empty pails are always lighter makes students aware of the need to think through a situation before making a snap decision. In deciding whether a pail is heavy, there is a combination of issues to consider—how heavy the empty pail is, but also the contents.

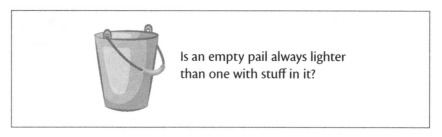

Is an empty pail always lighter than one with stuff in it?

OR

It is fun for students to think about giants. The activity below focuses on capacity. But it can be extended to focus on area, by considering the size of the plate a giant would use, or weight, by considering the weight of the food a giant would need.

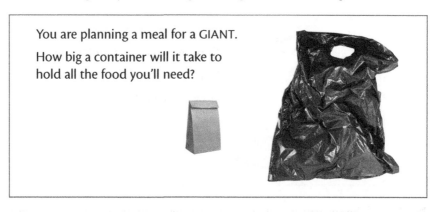

You are planning a meal for a GIANT.

How big a container will it take to hold all the food you'll need?

➤ You might read the book *Who Sank the Boat?* (Allen, 1982) to get into a discussion of weight. You might ask students why the boat got heavier and, perhaps, ask:

Which animal do you think sank the boat?

➤ Sorting and classifying are important activities for young children. Part of what they will do is compare the counts for the various groups they have created, but first they must think about how to sort. There are many sorting criteria students might use: kids who do or do not have sisters, kids who are wearing zippers or not, whether a student is wearing clothes with buttons or not, whether or not their boots are red, whether or not they are wearing black shoes, whether or not they have freckles, whether or not they can whistle, or whether or not they can say a tongue twister without getting twisted up.

Measurements can provide other sorting criteria. Aspects of student clothing can be sorted by length: shoes, pant legs, or shirt sleeves, for example. The activity below is based on hair length. Students will enjoy constructing pictures of themselves. Provide paper plates, markers or crayons, and yarn.

> Each of you use a paper plate to draw a picture of your face and attach hair. Use yarn to make the hair.
>
> Make your hair long if you have long hair and short if you have short hair.
>
> Let's look at all the pictures. How many more people have short hair than long?

OR

Provide a variety of items: some that float and some that sink, some that are made of plastic and some that are not, and some that are colorful and some that are not. This provides lots of criteria students can use for sorting, as shown below. For a different activity, you might also have children sort a number of heavy things, such as rocks, based on some other criteria.

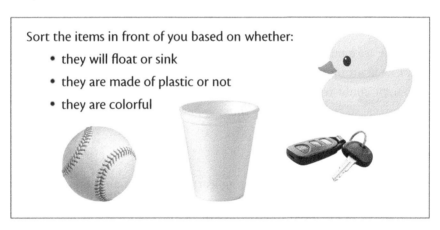

> Sort the items in front of you based on whether:
> - they will float or sink
> - they are made of plastic or not
> - they are colorful

➤ Provide interesting children's magazines that can be cut up. Have students choose pictures to cut out. Allowing them to decide on their own sorting criteria will give you great insight into what attributes different individuals attend to. They might sort the pictures by color, by product type, by size, and so forth.

> Choose a bunch of pictures from the magazines provided.
>
> Cut them out.
>
> Sort the pictures you cut out so that the groups you create are close to or exactly the same size.

Suggestions for Home Activities: Pre-K and Kindergarten

Make sure parents understand some of the critical underlying pieces of the math their children are learning. In particular, ensure that parents realize that their children are not yet measuring with units like inches.

➤ Encourage parents to raise measurement or data questions with their children. For example:

- If I squeeze the water out of each sponge into a different cup, which cup will be fuller?
- If I pop this popcorn, which bowl do you think we will need to hold it?
- Which of these boxes do you think will hold the most socks?
- How can we organize the knives, forks and spoons in a different way?

➤ Suggest that parents play "I spy" games with their children involving measurement. For example:

- I spy someone who is shorter than you.
- I spy something that is just a little longer than this pencil.
- I spy something that takes up more space than this placemat.
- I spy something that is heavier than this book.

➤ There are a number of measurement books parents can read with their children to provide an opportunity to have discussions about measurement. For example, a parent could read *The Grouchy Ladybug* (Carle, 1996a) and give clues about the animals, such as *Is it heavier than an ant? Is it longer than a dog?*

1st Grade

These activities provide engaging learning and practice opportunities.

➤ Students in 1st grade should have many opportunities to decide indirectly which of two items is longer. Generally that means using a third item to match with each of the two items that need to be compared. It is impossible to move classrooms, so the task below is an example where indirect measurement would be useful. Students might use a string in one room and move it to the next. Some students are likely to use units such as steps (in which case, you must encourage care with consistency of step size and no gaps or overlaps). If a wall is all windows, they might even use windows as their unit.

> Find a way to decide if your classroom or the classroom next door is longer.

OR

It is interesting to figure out where to go around the pumpkin in the activity below and for students to discover that it matters.

Predict whether it takes more string to go around this pumpkin if you go around the middle or if you go around from top to bottom.

OR

Provide a number of large turnips or other root vegetables. Read the book *The Enormous Turnip* (Baxter, 1994). Then set the task:

Which of these vegetables is widest?

How sure are you?

➤ Students at this grade level should be ordering more than two lengths. You might hang three pieces of string, one based on a particular child's leg length, one based on his or her arm length, and one based on his or her head **circumference**. Provide scissors and more string or yarn. It is likely that the child will compare his or her own leg length, arm length, or head circumference and extrapolate to this random person's lengths to deal with this task.

Look at the three strings. Decide which you think is a leg length, which is an arm length, and which is based on the distance around a head. Explain your thinking.

OR

Instead, you might ask students to compare other triples of lengths. Sports equipment might be of interest to children.

Which is usually longest? Shortest?

A child's hockey stick?   A child's baseball bat?   A child's golf club?

OR

Gather T-shirts labeled small, medium, and large. Lots of children like to use the words *small, medium,* and *large.* Here they have an opportunity to discover how these words apply in a real-life situation. Many adults might even wonder if there is a bigger difference between small and medium or between medium and large.

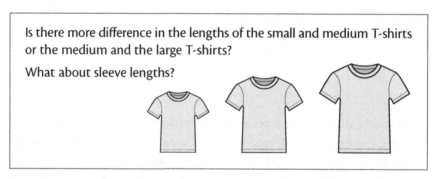

Is there more difference in the lengths of the small and medium T-shirts or the medium and the large T-shirts?

What about sleeve lengths?

➤ In 1st grade, students begin to use various nonstandard units to measure and to compare measurements. One of the most practical nonstandard units is our own step. Exploring giant steps and baby steps is interesting since students get to decide what is meant by each.

How many steps do you walk in a minute if you take regular steps?

What if you take giant steps?

What if you take baby steps?

OR

Usually when we have students measure to see the effect of unit size, we vary only the unit, and not the object being measured. One of the strengths of the activity below is that students have the opportunity to learn that the number of steps might be large EITHER because the giant step is big OR because the baby step is small. Similarly, the number of steps might be small EITHER because the giant step is not that big OR because the baby step is very big.

Some students are likely to use a "shuffle" to make a baby step, and they will get a big number. Some students might even compare areas rather than lengths.

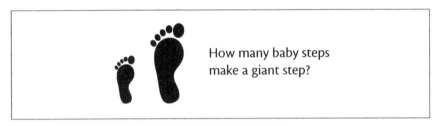

How many baby steps make a giant step?

> Students might explore the lengths of various exit routes they would take in case of a fire alarm and decide which route is shortest by measuring in nonstandard units. This is both practical and fun.

> Map out different exit routes you might take from your desk to the school side door.
>
> Measure, in steps, the lengths of those different routes and decide which is shortest.

OR

Tablet computers are attractive to children, so the suggestion below provides an opportunity to measure something of interest.

Measure your tablet in a unit of your choice.

Use your measurements, without the original tablet, to make a cover that is exactly the right size.

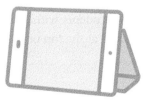

> It is useful to have students predict how many units long something might be. It develops their **spatial** and **proportional reasoning**. For example, you might provide only 3 paper clips to students and then ask:

> How many paper clips long, in total, do you think the book will be?
>
> Test your prediction.

OR

It turns out that no matter the size of a hoop, the distance it rolls would be a little more than three times its diameter. But students won't know this and they will have the opportunity to be surprised by what they discover.

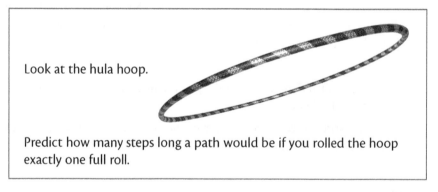

Look at the hula hoop.

Predict how many steps long a path would be if you rolled the hoop exactly one full roll.

> Knowing that different units lead to different measurements, you might provide a variety of units and ask students to predict which unit was used to achieve a certain result. For example, you might have measured your own arm with the black Cuisenaire rod. Provide many strips of paper (one per group) as long as your arm, although don't give them out until students are ready to test their predictions. Provide students with full sets of Cuisenaire rods and ask them to work on the task shown at the top of the next page.

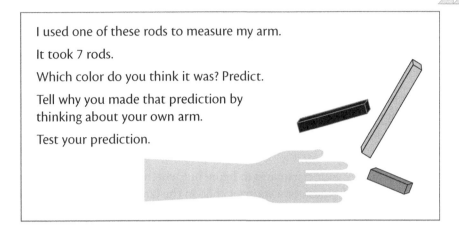

I used one of these rods to measure my arm.

It took 7 rods.

Which color do you think it was? Predict.

Tell why you made that prediction by thinking about your own arm.

Test your prediction.

> You might encourage students to develop personal "rulers" that allow them to measure items easily using nonstandard units. It is a matter of iterating a nonstandard unit many times and connecting the iterations. Provide strips of paper and markers. Constructing their own rulers will also provide children with a better understanding of how traditional rulers work.

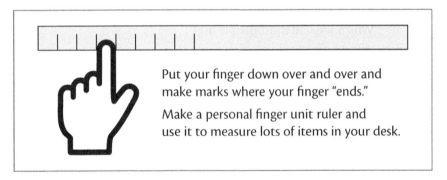

Put your finger down over and over and make marks where your finger "ends."

Make a personal finger unit ruler and use it to measure lots of items in your desk.

OR

A footprint ruler might be more useful for longer distances. The student might cut out a picture of his or her footprint to make the ruler.

Cut out a copy of your footprint.

Use it over and over, by attaching it to a string, with footprints touching, to make a footprint ruler. You can glue the footprints onto the string or punch holes and pull the string through the footprints.

Use your ruler to measure long things in the classroom.

➤ In 1st grade, students are expected to organize, represent, and interpret data. Interpreting data involves going beyond the details given to see other things that the data might reveal. Data collected might be about lots of things.

To facilitate data collection, you might provide information sheets children can use with names of classmates and boxes they can check for different answers. You might even have all children fill in information about a variety of topics that might be used for situations like the four presented below or others you might devise.

> Survey your classmates to figure out whether each child is the oldest, second-oldest, or a younger child in the family.
>
> Use your data to find out how many more (or fewer) kids in the class are first-born than not.

OR

> Ask your classmates about the last time they or a friend or family member traveled to or from another city.
>
> Find out if the traveler went by car, by plane, or some other way.
>
> Which way did most people use?
>
> Which way did the fewest people use?
>
> How many more used the first way than the second?

OR

> Ask your classmates whether they would rather attend an event that involves sports, music, or dance.
>
> Tell some things you learned about your classmates from that information.

OR

Ask your classmates whether they live in an apartment building, in a house close to other houses, or in a house far from other houses.

Tell some things you learned about where your classmates live from that information.

➤ You might integrate a "probability experiment" with data collection and sorting. Provide a paper bag with 10 cubes of different colors in it. Tell students that after they take a cube out and note its color, to put it back in the bag and shake up the cubes. This activity encourages mathematical reasoning; 10 cubes and 20 draws were used to force the reasoning.

Choose a cube from the bag. Note the color and put the cube back in the bag.

Choose 20 cubes altogether.

First, tell some things you noticed about the colors.

Predict how many of each color are in the bag if there are only 10 cubes in it.

Check to see if you are right.

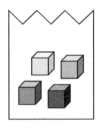

Suggestions for Home Activities: 1st Grade

You might encourage parents to come to school for a "fun math at home" program or create short videos for them and post them on your school website. Make sure parents are familiar with and comfortable with the kinds of math activities their children are performing in school. You might create a blog with short postings or videos where you model or talk about some of the math activities in which their children are engaging.

➤ Encourage parents to support length comparisons by having them ask their children questions like the ones below, as appropriate.

- Which is longer, the couch in the living room or the couch downstairs?
- Which is longer, your bed or the couch?
- Which looks bigger around—that grapefruit or this orange?
- How many steps would it take to visit each room in our house (or apartment) starting at the front door?
- Which string bean do you think is the longest?

➤ Make sure parents know that children in 1st grade are focused on hour and half-hour times, although some children might be ready for more. Encourage parents to have their children tell them what time it is at these hour and half-hour markings by looking at a clock (whether digital or analog) in the house.

➤ There are many opportunities at home to practice sorting. Suggest to parents that they have children help them sort clothes (e.g., based on to whom they belong or whether they must be hung or not), sort food to put it away (e.g., in pantry or fridge or freezer), sort toys to put them away, and so forth. Parents might even have their child sort all the people at a family event in different ways (e.g., babies, children, and grown-ups; people I see a lot vs. people I hardly ever see; etc.).

2nd Grade

These activities provide engaging learning and practice opportunities.

➤ Students need many experiences measuring with standard units to become comfortable being able to estimate lengths, heights, and distances in everyday situations. For example, you might help students get a sense of 1 meter by providing appropriate materials and asking them to make estimates like these:

Estimate numbers that make sense for each situation and check your estimates.
- A line of _____ pencils would make a meter.
- A line of _____ toothpicks would make a meter.
- A line of _____ toothbrushes would make a meter.
- A line of _____ straws would make a meter.

Make up other lines you could add to the list.

OR

Students might get a sense of a variety of units by completing a task like the one below. You will need to provide the appropriate materials.

Write appropriate measurements in each blank.

Estimate first and then check.

- A line of 10 pencils would be _____ long.
- A line of 10 toothpicks would be _____ long.
- A line of 10 rulers would be _____ long.
- A line of 10 straws would be _____ long.

Add some other items to this list.

OR

Choose 8 items in the classroom.

- Some need to be a lot more than 1 yard long.
- Some need to be a lot shorter than 1 foot long.
- Some need to be about 30 inches long.

➢ Students might look for pairs of items that are specific distances apart. This involves multiple measurements.

Find two items that are about these distances apart.

- 1 inch   • 5 inches   • 10 inches

Predict first and then check your predictions.

➢ Students might enjoy having measurement competitions with other children. The idea of a cotton puff flick is suggested here, but distance could also be ball throws or any other distance that could be reasonably achieved in the classroom.

Join a group of 3 other children.

Have a competition with other groups to see whose total distance is greatest if each person in the group flicks a cotton puff and measures (in inches) how far it goes; the group value is the total of all 4 distances.

➤ Sometimes we tell a person how loud (or quiet) they should be by saying something like "Use a 12-inch voice. That would mean that nobody beyond 12 inches away could hear what is being said. A voice-related task might be:

> How far away can somebody hear you when you whisper?
>
> How far away can somebody hear you when you speak in a regular "loudness"?
>
> How far away can somebody hear you when you shout?

➤ It might be interesting for students to think about how long something is that is zigzagged, like shoelaces, or something that can stretch, like elastic.

> How long are your shoelaces?
>
> How many inches of material is used to make both of your laces?

OR

> How long do you think a 6" piece of elastic will stretch?
>
> Check your prediction.

➤ Students might enjoy the mystery of thinking about a line plot in reverse. You show the plot and then ask children what they think was measured. An example is shown at the top of the next page.

Andrew measured 10 items in the classroom in inches.

He made a line plot to show the results.

What items do you think Andrew might have measured?

Numbers of Items

```
                                    X
                                    X
                                    X
        X                           X
        X                           X
        X       X                   X
   _____
        6   7   8   9   10  11  12   Inches
```

Does this prove that there are more items that are 12" long than 6" long in the classroom?

> Students need to associate various times of day with events.

Choose 4 times of the day.

Write the times and show what they look like on an analog (round) clock.

Don't forget a.m. or p.m.

Draw pictures to show what you might be doing at each of the times.

> Students need to think about what the hands of the clock look like at different times of day.

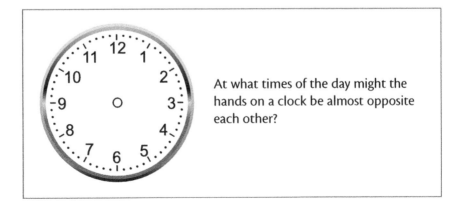

At what times of the day might the hands on a clock be almost opposite each other?

➤ Students are expected to become familiar with the look and value of pennies, nickels, dimes, and quarters and expected to solve problems involving these coins. A number of such problems are provided below.

Grab a handful of coins.

Estimate the value and check.

OR

Show different ways to make 50¢.

OR

How much could 8 coins be worth if there is at least one penny, one nickel, one dime, and one quarter?

➤ You might also use problems where students use addition or subtraction in a money context. For example, you might provide a menu with items and prices and pose a situation like the one below.

Choose 3 items to buy.

How much change would you get if you gave the restaurant 100¢?

My Menu	
Drinks	10¢
Soup	20¢
Sandwiches	25¢
Veggies with Dip	15¢
Fruit	30¢
Cheese	15¢
Dessert	20¢

➤ There are many opportunities for students to make concrete graphs involving themselves. Students can sort themselves into groups based on the criteria listed below as well as others, for example, whether they have sisters or not, whether they live near their grandparents or not, and so forth.

Students could make sure they line up 1-1, or you might provide them with a large piece of plastic with squares on which they can stand. The plastic needs two columns, as shown below.

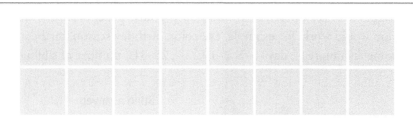

Make a human graph with your classmates.

Line up in rows matched 1-1 with a classmate, or on squares in one row or the other, depending on whether:

• You are a boy or a girl, *or*

• You have curly hair or not, *or*

• You are wearing red today or not, *or*

• You come to school on a bus or not.

➤ Students might enjoy thinking about the weather and using that to create a graph.

Create a weather graph using umbrellas for rainy days, a sun for sunny days, and a cloud for cloudy days to show the weather last week.

What conclusions can you make?

➤ Students might find out information about their classmates through surveys and create picture graphs that compare the students using various criteria. Two ideas are shown, but there are many other possibilities, for examples, favorite pizza toppings, favorite colors, whether children have brothers or not, and so forth.

Create a picture graph comparing how many students wore a hat to school today to how many did not.

What conclusions can you make?

OR

> Create a picture graph comparing kids' favorite desserts.
>
> What conclusions can you make?

➤ A bar graph is one of the more familiar graph types for students since they encounter frequent examples in the media. Because there are so many ways to sort items that occur in the environment, the number of topics for bar graphs is vast. Some suggestions are offered below and on the next page, but easily determined criterion would work: for example, eye color, birthday season, birthdate categorized in some fashion (e.g., days 1–5, 2–10, . . . , 26–31), number of siblings, and so forth.

> Build a tower.
>
> Make a bar graph to show how many of each different type of block you used.
>
> What could someone learn about your tower from the bar graph?

OR

> Find out favorite breakfast foods of some of your classmates.
>
> Show that information in a bar graph.
>
> What could someone learn about favorite breakfast foods from the graph?

OR

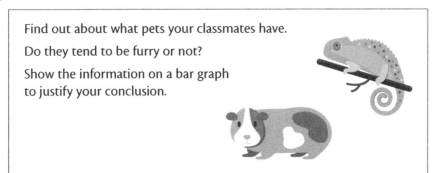

Find out about what pets your classmates have.

Do they tend to be furry or not?

Show the information on a bar graph
to justify your conclusion.

Suggestions for Home Activities: 2nd Grade

You might encourage parents to come to school for a "fun math at home" program or create short videos for them and post them on your school website. Make sure parents are familiar with and comfortable with the kinds of math activities their children are performing in school. You might create a blog with short postings or videos where you model or talk about some of the math activities in which their children are engaging.

Make sure parents understand the importance of probing and questioning rather than showing their children how to do something.

> Encourage parents to find opportunities to have their children help them measure using inches, feet, centimeters, or meters. It might be how long cucumbers or beans tend to be, how long rooms are, how tall people in the family are, how long furniture is, and so forth.

> Have parents (or help them) develop a concentration card game where students match digital clock times with corresponding analog clock times. They might also stop their children occasionally near a clock (digital or analog) and have the child read the time.

> Parents might read a book like *It's About Time!* (Murphy, 2005) or *What Time Is It, Mr. Crocodile?* (Sierra, 2007) or *The Clock Struck One* (Harris, 2009) and talk with their children about events that occur in their home at various times of day.

> Encourage parents to create a family graph showing how many minutes a week each member of the family spends reading.

❖ CHAPTER 6 ❖

Geometry

THIS CHAPTER focuses on geometric and spatial concepts young students explore in Pre-K through Grade 2.

THE FUNDAMENTALS

The field of geometry includes the study of shapes (1-dimensional, 2-dimensional, and 3-dimensional) as well as **spatial relationships**, which encompass positional relationships and attribute relationships among shapes.

What Aspects of Geometry Do Primary Students Meet?

In the Common Core curriculum (2010), primary grade students consider positional relationships, learn definitions of various shapes (particularly squares, circles, rectangles, triangles, pentagons, trapezoids, and half and quarter circles, as well as cubes, cones, cylinders, rectangular prisms, and spheres), and explore the attributes of those shapes. They also **partition** and compose shapes and explore where they see shapes in the world. They draw and build shapes as well.

Long-standing research has described a taxonomy of development in geometry. The most famous formulation of this work is called the Van Hiele Taxonomy of Geometric Thought (Teppo, 1991). Primary students generally work at Level 0: Visualization into Level 1: Analysis.

Recent research has made it clear that young students can do much more in geometry than they are currently being asked to do, and they enjoy doing it (Caswell, 2013), Most of the activities listed here focus on what the curriculum calls for, but there is a section at the end of the chapter with appropriate additional geometry activities.

Positional Vocabulary

Most children come to school with some knowledge of **positional vocabulary**, particularly words like *under, over, near, far, inside,* and *outside.* They should also meet words and phrases such as *above, below, beside, in front of,* and *behind.*

Part of the issue with positional words is that they are relative; what one person regards as *far,* another might not. Even words like *above* and *below* can be tricky. Some students believe *above* means directly above, whereas others believe that the ceiling light is above them even if they are not immediately under it.

Many positional words are opposites; *far* and *near* are opposites, as are *above* and *below,* or *in front of* and *behind.* It might be helpful to create word wall pictures that show some of these pairs. For example:

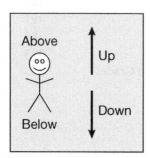 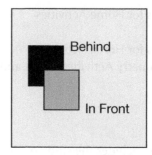 

2-D Shapes

One-dimensional shapes are lines, **line segments**, and **rays**. Students use these terms, especially *lines,* informally, but do not study them in any depth until they are older. However, students do study 2-dimensional shapes, which are flat and lie on **planes**, and 3-dimensional shapes, which are concrete and not flat.

➤ *What Are 2-D Shapes?*

Students will meet many 2-dimensional shapes. Earliest, they encounter squares, circles, rectangles, **triangles**, and **hexagons**.

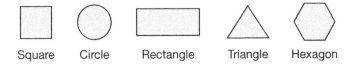

A bit later they also meet **trapezoids, pentagons, parallelograms,** other **quadrilaterals**, half-circles, and quarter-circles.

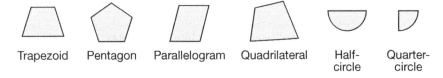

At this stage, students may not realize that squares can be rectangles, which they will learn later. However, there is an advantage in calling a rectangle a non-square rectangle, at least some of the time, to make the transition easier later.

It is important that students meet these shapes in various orientations and sizes. For example, students need to realize that the shapes below are rectangles or triangles.

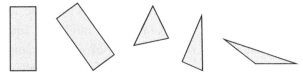

In particular, triangles should not always be **equilateral** or **isosceles** and should sometimes have **obtuse angles,** as shown above.

Students need to understand which features are critical for particular shapes. The activity at the top of the next page is for triangles, but similar activities can be created for rectangles or cubes or circles. The shapes illustrated in the activity were selected because students might, for example, not distinguish triangular prisms from triangles, might not think about the need for the shape to be closed, might be affected by orientation, or might think that if any part of a shape is triangular, the shape is a triangle.

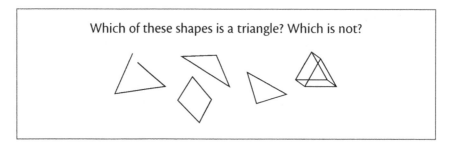

Students need to use attributes to compare two shapes. In the activity below, triangles are used, but the activity can also be used with two versions of a rectangular prism or with a circle and a sphere or perhaps with a square and a circle.

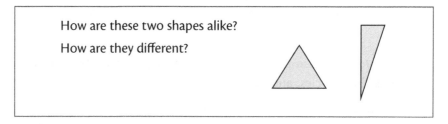

It is useful to introduce language like *side,* **vertex**, and *angle* so that students can be precise in their descriptions of shapes.

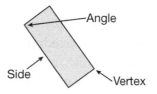

> **Where Do We See 2-D Shapes?**

Students should explore where they see shapes (or close approximations of them) in their everyday world. For example, we might see squares as tiles, circles as maintenance hole covers, rectangles as book covers, triangles as traffic signs, and hexagons as tiles. We see pentagon shapes on soccer balls, trapezoids as the shape of some tabletops, and half-circles and quarter-circles as parts of pizzas.

Square

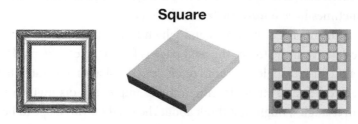

Circle

Rectangle

Triangle

Hexagon

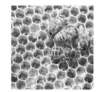 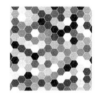

Pentagon

Trapezoid

➤ *Defining Attributes Versus Nondefining Attributes*

Every shape has attributes (i.e., characteristics). With respect to a shape, its attributes might be its color, whether its edges are rounded, whether it has equal sides, how many sides it has, whether it has **reflective symmetry**, whether it has sides that are **parallel** (will never touch, no matter how far they might be extended), or whether the shape is **convex** (has no "dents").

Some attributes of a shape define the shape (**defining attributes**) and some do not. For example, knowing the color of a shape does not define that shape, but knowing it is **closed** and has straight sides defines it as a polygon. Knowing that a closed shape has four straight equal sides and at least one **right angle** defines it as a square, but knowing simply that it has at least four equal sides does not define it at all (since it might have additional nonequal sides or even curved sides). Symmetry is never a defining attribute, but it is an attribute. (Students do not formally study symmetry in the Common Core curriculum, 2010, until 4th grade.)

Students in 1st grade are expected to distinguish between defining attributes and attributes that are less essential to classifying a shape.

* A square is a closed shape with four straight equal sides and four **square corners**. It turns out that even though a square has four square corners, knowing that there is one square corner, when the shape already is known to be a quadrilateral with equal sides, forces the other corners to be square as well.

    Knowing that there are four square vertices, or corners, does not define a square, since rectangles that are not square also have four square corners. Knowing that there are four equal sides does not define a square, since rhombuses that are not squares also have four equal sides.

* A circle is a closed shape where all the points on the edge are equally distant from one center point.

    Knowing that a shape is round is too vague to define a circle, since this is also true of other shapes, such as **ellipses**.

* A rectangle is a closed shape with four straight sides, at least one square corner, and opposite sides that are equal.

    Knowing that opposite sides are parallel, as opposed to equal, and that there are four straight sides with at least one square corner also defines a rectangle.

    Many children think there needs to be a longer side for a shape to be a rectangle, but that is not true, since squares are rectangles. Similarly, many children think that the length should be about double the width, but, again, this is not required.

- A triangle is a closed shape with three straight sides. The lengths of the sides and sizes of the angles are not relevant to determining whether the shape is a triangle.

  Another way to define a triangle is as a closed shape with straight sides and exactly three vertices.

- A hexagon is a closed shape with six straight sides. The lengths of the sides and sizes of the angles are not relevant to determining whether the shape is a hexagon.

- A pentagon is a closed shape with five straight sides. The lengths of the sides and sizes of the angles are not relevant to determining whether the shape is a pentagon.

- A trapezoid is a closed shape with four straight sides and with two of those sides parallel (not touching, even if extended). Knowing the lengths of the sides and sizes of the angles is not relevant to determining whether the shape is a trapezoid.

  Some mathematicians define a trapezoid as a quadrilateral having *exactly* one pair of parallel sides, and others define it as having *at least* one pair of parallel sides, making a parallelogram a type of trapezoid for those latter individuals.

Learning about defining and nondefining attributes can be approached in a number of ways; one is shown in the activity below. Students might reuse the activity repeatedly by choosing a different shape.

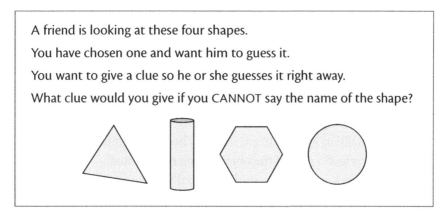

A friend is looking at these four shapes.
You have chosen one and want him to guess it.
You want to give a clue so he or she guesses it right away.
What clue would you give if you CANNOT say the name of the shape?

Primary students will deal with only simple attributes, such as whether the shape has curved or only straight sides, how many sides or corners it has, whether the sides are all equal or not, or whether or not there is symmetry.

➤ *How Are 2-D Shapes Alike and Different?*

Shapes can be similar or different based on any attributes, whether defining attributes or not. When students compare shapes, attention should be given, as much as possible, to geometric attributes such as numbers of sides, side length comparisons, and types of angles, rather than to features like size or color, but students will notice both.

Students might just choose one shape and think of another shape they feel is different from it but still a lot like it.

What shape do you think is not a square, but a lot like it?

➤ *Drawing 2-D Shapes*

Students should have opportunities to draw shapes. Likely tracing the shapes at first is wise, but then students should try to represent 2-D shapes by exploring them visually and sketching.

The pictures are not meant to be perfect representations but will give a teacher insight into what a student is noticing about a shape.

➤ *Composing and Partitioning Shapes*

Clements (2004) has laid out what he believes are the stages students go through in combining (composing) and partitioning (decomposing) shapes.

- Clements talks about the pre-composer stage, where children use various shapes, separately, to represent objects. They don't worry about shape or size. These tend to be preschool children.
- Then children build pictures with shapes, and the various shapes represent various parts of the picture. These tend to be preschool children or kindergarten students.
- Usually in kindergarten, students begin to combine several shapes to represent a part of the object being represented.
- Still in kindergarten, students usually think about how shapes fit together as they build their pictures.
- In subsequent primary years, children form composite shapes and even substitute some shapes for others.
- Then, usually still in the primary years, children create designs where a unit is intentionally repeated.

Composing. Students combine shapes to create other shapes. For example, they might put together a square and a triangle to make a house shape. Or they might put together two squares to make a rectangle or a square and a triangle to make a trapezoid.

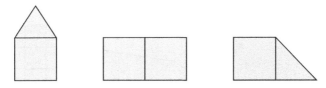

There might be some children who notice that every shape is composed of smaller shapes. For example, the large square below is made up of 4 small squares; the hexagon is made of six triangles.

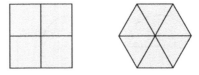

In 1st grade, students compose shapes to make other shapes. A 2-D set of shapes is used in the activity below, but 3-D shapes can also be used.

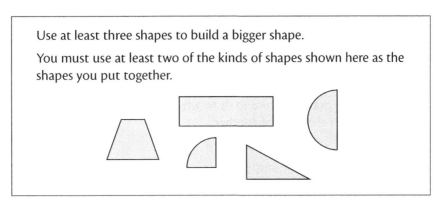

Use at least three shapes to build a bigger shape.

You must use at least two of the kinds of shapes shown here as the shapes you put together.

Partitioning. Partitioning shapes involves breaking them up into parts. Partitioning is important in later work in geometry. For example, later we partition a parallelogram into a rectangle and two triangles to come up with a formula for area, or we partition a hexagon into triangles to figure out the angle sizes.

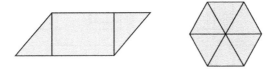

There are lots of opportunities for students to explore what happens when various shapes are broken into other shapes. Students should realize that all shapes can be partitioned or decomposed into other shapes. For example, every straight-sided closed shape can be decomposed into triangles and every square can be decomposed into smaller squares.

More specifically, in the Common Core curriculum (2010), the concept of one-half and one-quarter are introduced by using partitioning of circles and rect-angles. Below, each gray section is half or a quarter of its whole shape.

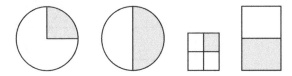

Students need to learn that quarters of the same whole are always smaller than halves of that whole. They might explore, though, that quarters of one whole are not necessarily smaller than halves of another.

Draw a picture to show why a quarter of a shape is always less than half of that shape.

Then draw a picture to show why a quarter of one shape might be bigger than half of another.

It is important for students to realize that fractional parts need to have the same area, but not necessarily be **congruent**.

Which of these rectangles is divided into quarters? Which is not? Explain.

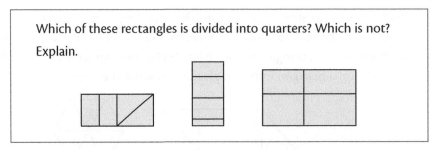

In 2nd grade, students also learn to partition rectangles into other numbers of equal parts, based on rows and columns. For example, the fraction one-sixth is visible in the diagram below.

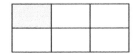

To get students to think about partitioning a rectangle into equal rows and columns, you might ask the following:

> You have partitioned a rectangle into exactly 12 identical pieces.
>
> How might you have done that?
>
> Show with this rectangle.
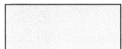

3-D Shapes

➤ What Are 3-D Shapes?

3-D shapes that primary students meet are likely to be cubes, spheres, cylinders, **rectangular prisms**, and cones.

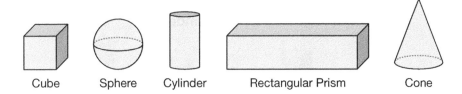

Cube   Sphere   Cylinder   Rectangular Prism   Cone

Students should learn some of the vocabulary we attach to 3-D shapes. We call the corners vertices and the flat "sides" of the shape **faces**; the line segments where faces meet are called **edges**.

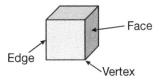

Just as with 2-D shapes, students should meet 3-D shapes in a variety of sizes and orientations. For example, a rectangular prism might be tilted.

➤ *Where Do We See 3-D Shapes?*

The shapes (or close approximations of them) primary grade children study are visible in everyday life. Students should look for these shapes around them. For example, they might see a cube or a rectangular prism as a cardboard box, a sphere as a ball, a cylinder as a food can, or a cone as what holds their ice cream. Parents and educators identifying objects like books, globes, balls, blocks, and paper towel or toilet paper rolls by their shape names prompts children to notice and name them frequently too. This reinforces children's learning and can be fun for both the children and their family members. Other examples are:

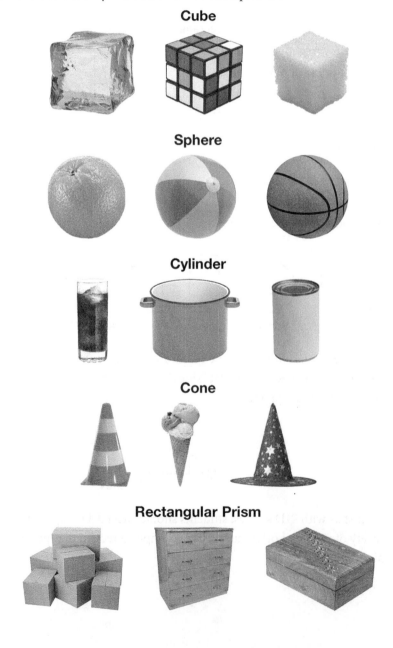

Cube

Sphere

Cylinder

Cone

Rectangular Prism

> *Defining Attributes Versus Nondefining Attributes*

Students might consider different attributes of 3-D shapes. They might look at non-defining attributes like color or orientation, or they might think about defining attributes. For example, what makes a sphere a sphere is the defining attribute that every point on the surface is an equal distance from the center point. What makes a cylinder a cylinder is the defining attribute that it is a closed surface where the top and bottom, called **bases**, are congruent circles, as is every **cross-section** cut parallel to a base. What makes a cube a cube is that its six faces are congruent squares, with three faces meeting at each vertex. What makes a cone a cone is that there is a curved surface with a circle base tapering to a point called the **apex**. What makes a rectangular prism a rectangular prism is that all of the faces are rectangles, 3 faces meet at each vertex, and each pair of opposite faces is congruent.

Students in 2nd grade begin to think about the components of 3-D shapes. You might ask the question below to focus students on the notion that opposite faces of rectangular prisms are congruent and that cubes are rectangular prisms.

> You are looking at a rectangular prism.
>
> How many faces might it have that are EXACTLY the same?

[*Possible solutions:* 2 or 4 (if the base is square but it's not a cube) or 6 (for a cube).]

> *How Are 3-D Shapes Alike and Different?*

3-D shapes can be similar or different based on any of their attributes, whether they are defining attributes or not. When students compare shapes, as much as possible, attention should be given to geometric attributes like numbers of faces, shapes of faces, or whether there are faces or curved surfaces, rather than other attributes such as color or size.

> *Building 3-D Shapes*

Students might try to build 3-D shapes using either plasticine shaped more or less like the shape or else by building a **skeleton** using, for example, toothpicks and mini-marshmallows.

Students can create skeletons of other 3-D shapes if provided straws or tooth-picks and molding clay in which to insert the straws or toothpicks. They should think about what they need to do before they begin to build.

> Use the toothpicks and clay to build a model for a rectangular prism.
>
> What did you have to do to make sure the model is a good one?

Some children might enjoy making **face maps** of a rectangular prism by draw-ing, separately, each face. They might notice that there are always three pairs of identical faces (sometimes more) and that all of the faces are rectangles. Some students might even notice that each rectangle has at least one dimension in com-mon with other rectangles that are not identical to it.

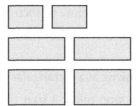

➤ Composing 3-D Shapes

Students might also put together shapes to build interesting objects. For example, they might put a rectangular prism and cube together to build a new shape, or they might use a rectangular prism with a cylinder.

MISCONCEPTIONS TO WATCH FOR

➤ *Misunderstandings About Terms Like Above, Below, Beside.* Some children believe that there are constraints on positional words that others do not feel. For example, for some children, a cloud is only *above* you if you are directly under it; for other children, it is above you regardless of where you are on the ground.

The same is true for a term like *below* or *beside,* where some children are more sensitive than others to what the distance between the items needs to be.

➤ *Not Recognizing Shapes When Orientation Changes.* Many children believe that the first shape below is a triangle, but the others are not. They would argue that the second shape is an upside down triangle (not a real triangle) and the third isn't a triangle at all.

The only way for students to learn that this is not true is for the teacher or parent to regularly show triangles in unusual orientations or regularly show children different types of triangles.

> *Incorrectly Using 2-D Vocabulary to Describe 3-D Objects.* Many children call spheres circles or call cubes squares because they often hear adults do that. It is important for parents and teachers to be as correct with vocabulary as possible so students can mimic proper vocabulary usage.

> *Difficulty Counting Edges, Vertices, or Faces of a 3-D Shape.* Because it is hard to keep track, students often make mistakes when trying to count all of the edges, vertices, or faces of a 3-D shape. It is a good idea to provide small stickers that children can attach to a component of a shape once they have counted it.

THE FUN

Pre-K and Kindergarten

These activities provide engaging learning and practice opportunities.

> There are many opportunities for students to practice the use of positional vocabulary. You might need to model an example of an instruction for the suggested activity below. For example: Simon says *Put your right hand below your left hand.* Or: Simon says *Put your left foot ahead of your right foot.*

> Play a game of Simon Says.
>
> One of you is Simon and gives instructions that involve words like *above, below, beside, up,* and *down.*
>
> Others follow the instructions.
>
> Remember to catch someone who moves when you do not say "Simon says."

OR

You might sing the *Hokey Pokey* song with your students, with them doing the motions, putting arms in and out, and so on.

> Let's sing the *Hokey Pokey* song together.

OR

Provide toy farm equipment, such as a barn, a silo, farm animals, and so forth. Make sure there is also a fence that can serve as a corral.

Arrange your farm equipment and animals so that you can describe the scene you create.

But you have to be able to use these words: *beside, near, inside, outside,* and *above.*

➤ Children can go on shape hunts either around the school, inside the classroom, or outside. You might give students a checklist with a space to indicate where they found the object in question and a space to sketch it. Or they might use digital devices to take photographs or narrate videos describing the locations.

Look for these shapes around us:

- Triangle, rectangle, square, circle, hexagon
- Sphere, cone, cube, cylinder

➤ Students can be creative and imagine situations involving shapes. A few examples are given in the activity below, but you can create others, for example, all circles disappear or become triangles, or all cubes are changed to spheres. Students might choose which of these they would prefer to consider.

How would your life change if:

- Every room in your house became a cylinder? *OR*
- Every square turned into a rectangle that was not a square? *OR*
- Every rectangle became a square? *OR*
- Every cylinder became a cone?

> In the task below, children form shapes with their own bodies (e.g., 4 children form a square).

Alternatively, students could be given a loop of yarn and they would work together, positioning themselves with one finger hooked into the loop to form vertices of a shape they are trying to create.

It would be interesting to see how children approach creating a circle. It is not really possible with bodies lying on the ground, but students may realize they can come close by curving their bodies or using lots and lots of people. Or students might choose to ignore the suggestion of lying on the ground and might choose to pretend there is a circle and just stand up on points around the circle.

In the right size group, arrange your bodies lying on the floor to form:

• A square   • A rectangle not a square   • A triangle

Can you form a circle?

> Students might create 3-D shapes or 2-D shapes in a sandbox. You might provide boxes and cylindrical pails they could fill or could use to make impressions in the sand. Alternatively, you might provide cookie cutters or pattern blocks to serve as molds.

What shapes can you create using the sand?

➤ Students might consider attributes of shapes in different ways. In the activity below, they think about changing just one attribute.

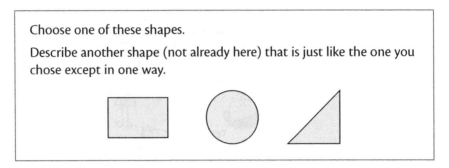

Choose one of these shapes.

Describe another shape (not already here) that is just like the one you chose except in one way.

➤ Students consider attributes when they sort or create patterns. Provide students with a variety of shapes to consider; they could be 2-D or 3-D or a mixture. Many combinations are possible.

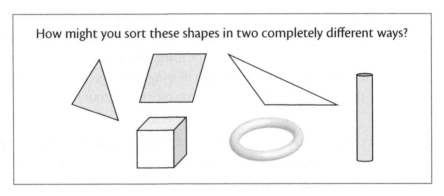

How might you sort these shapes in two completely different ways?

➤ Students can use a variety of attributes of shapes to help them build patterns. Pattern identification and creation is an important part of early childhood learning in math. Patterns are based on identification of attributes.

Create a repeating pattern that follows one of these rules:

- Rolls, doesn't roll, rolls, doesn't roll, . . .
- Triangle, not triangle, triangle, not triangle, triangle, not triangle, . . .
- Circle, circle, sphere, sphere, circle, circle, sphere, sphere, . . .

> You might use the book *Which One Doesn't Belong: A Shapes Book* (Danielson, 2017) to have students explore how shapes are alike and different.

Four shapes are shown and students decide which one doesn't belong. There is always more than one possibility, depending on the attribute being considered. Here is such a situation:

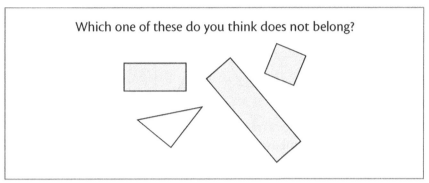

Which one of these do you think does not belong?

[*Possible solutions:* The white shape since it is the only white one, the top left rectangle since it is the only one not tilted, or the square since it is the only one with all equal sides.]

> Provide square tiles to allow students to notice that you can't always make bigger squares from smaller ones; only certain numbers of uniform smaller squares can be combined to create larger squares.

Build a larger square using identical square tiles.

How many tiles could you use?

How many could you NOT use?

[*Possible solutions:* 4 or 9 or 16 . . . are possible; 2, 3, 5, 6, 7, . . . are not.]

> Students might build larger cubes from smaller linking cubes. They could explore how many cubes it takes to build larger cubes.

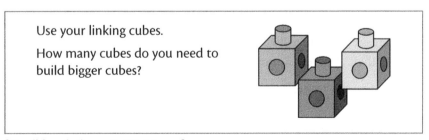

Use your linking cubes.

How many cubes do you need to build bigger cubes?

[*Possible solutions:* 8, 27, 64, ...]

> Students might use pattern block shapes to make other shapes. This gives them practice composing in an enjoyable way.

Use 2 pattern block shapes to make a different pattern block shape.

Use 3 pattern block shapes to make a different pattern block shape.

Use 6 pattern block shapes to make a different pattern block shape.

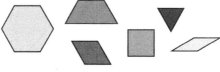

[*Possible solutions:* 2 trapezoids make a hexagon or 2 triangles make a rhombus; 3 rhombuses make a hexagon or 3 triangles make a trapezoid; 6 triangles make a hexagon.]

Suggestions for Home Activities: Pre-K and Kindergarten

Make sure parents understand some of the critical underlying pieces of the math their children are learning. Let parents know the shapes their children are working with.

> Encourage parents to have children show them shapes by tracing them in the air.

> Have parents hide a shape in a paper bag and ask their children, just by feeling and not looking, to decide which shape it is.

> Parents could go on shape hunts with their children looking for 2-D and 3-D shapes around the house, in the supermarket, in the car, and so on.

> Parents could build structures with building blocks with their children. The child hides his or her eyes while the parent makes one change in the structure. The child opens his or her eyes and tries to figure out what has changed.

> There are a number of children's books focused on shape. Parents might read these with their children. Some examples are:

> *Shapes That Roll* (Nagel, 2009)
> *Shapes, Shapes, Shapes* (Hoban, 1996)
> *Mouse Shapes* (Walsh, 2007)

1st Grade

These activities provide engaging learning and practice opportunities. Because the geometry curriculum is fairly light in 1st and 2nd grades, there are some additional activities at the end of the 2nd-grade activities focused on symmetry, partitioning, and spatial visualization that you might want to add to the content you teach.

➤ Students in 1st grade might create riddles so that other children can guess a shape they are thinking of. You might show them what riddles sound like before they begin. For example: *A lot of soup cans look like me.* Or: *You might throw me.*

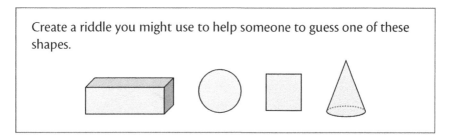

Create a riddle you might use to help someone to guess one of these shapes.

OR

You might help students focus on various attributes of shapes by giving them a task like this one:

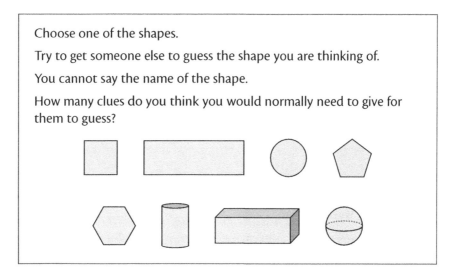

Choose one of the shapes.

Try to get someone else to guess the shape you are thinking of.

You cannot say the name of the shape.

How many clues do you think you would normally need to give for them to guess?

➤ Many activities that involve putting shapes together are useful to help students to gain a better understanding of the space in which they live. For example, the task at the top of the next page challenges students to use pattern blocks to try to create animals.

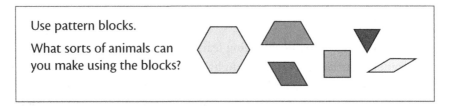

Use pattern blocks.

What sorts of animals can you make using the blocks?

OR

It could go the other way, where you give students pieces of traditional shapes and they must figure out what shape they came from.

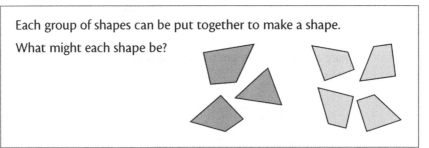

Each group of shapes can be put together to make a shape.

What might each shape be?

[*Possible solutions:* For example, isosceles triangle and regular hexagon.]

OR

You might provide pattern block shapes and ask a question like the one below. You could vary the activity by using shapes that are not triangles, or using a specific mix of shapes (e.g., 2 triangles and 4 thin rhombuses). This type of exploration helps students see better how shapes go together.

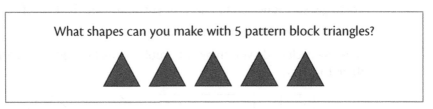

What shapes can you make with 5 pattern block triangles?

OR

This activity is for fun, but it helps students focus on how to decompose shapes in interesting ways.

At your next birthday, you are going to turn 7.

You want to design a birthday cake that looks like a 7 by putting together other shapes.

What shapes would you put together to make your cake?

> Students might solve shape puzzles. You can put together a variety of shapes using pattern block pieces and the children must figure out where the pieces go.

There are different levels of difficulty you might use. For some students, you should show all internal lines so it is fairly obvious which shape goes where. For other students, you should show just the outline. For yet other students, you might reduce or enlarge the outline so that they can test only visually and not physically.

The same simple puzzle is shown three ways here:

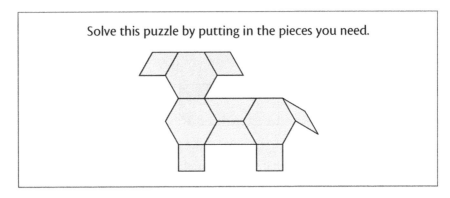

Solve this puzzle by putting in the pieces you need.

OR

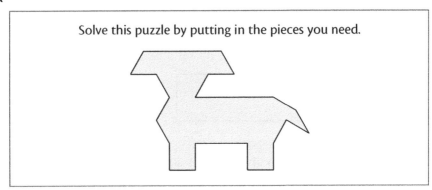

Solve this puzzle by putting in the pieces you need.

OR

Solve this puzzle by putting in the pieces you need.

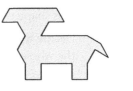

➤ Students might compose 3-D shapes to build new shapes and put them together to make structures. The new shapes they create can even be given names.

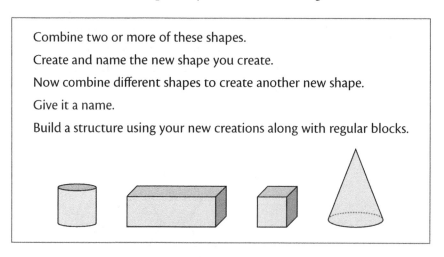

Combine two or more of these shapes.

Create and name the new shape you create.

Now combine different shapes to create another new shape.

Give it a name.

Build a structure using your new creations along with regular blocks.

➤ Students should realize that there is usually more than one way to halve or quarter a rectangle, so you might ask the question below. You can facilitate the work by providing multiple copies of each shape.

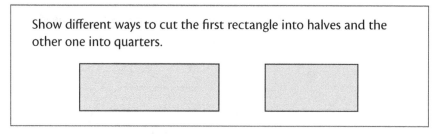

Show different ways to cut the first rectangle into halves and the other one into quarters.

➤ Sometimes it is useful to give students a part and have them imagine the whole. Being able to go both ways (from whole to part or part to whole) will later support fraction learning.

This shape is a fraction of another shape.

Decide what the fraction is and show what the whole might look like.

Are you sure?

Suggestions for Home Activities: 1st Grade

You might encourage parents to come to school for a "fun math at home" program or create short videos for them and post them on your school website. You might create a blog with short postings or videos where you model or talk about some of the math activities in which their children are engaging.

➤ Encourage parents to support geometry learning at home by building 3-D structures with their children based on cylinders, rectangular prisms, and cones. They should have their children use as much geometry vocabulary as possible to describe what they have created.

➤ Encourage parents to use pattern block apps with their child to compose shapes online.

➤ Encourage parents, when they cut cakes or pies or other food items into halves or quarters, to have the child name the fractional parts.

➤ It is always valuable to encourage parents to build spatial sense in their children by doing jigsaw puzzles with them or by letting them see simple drawings or shape structures for short periods and asking them to recreate them.

2nd Grade

These activities provide engaging learning and practice opportunities. Because the geometry curriculum is fairly light in 1st and 2nd grades, there are some additional activities at the end of the 2nd-grade activities focused on symmetry, partitioning, and spatial visualization that you might want to add to the content you teach.

➤ To practice recognizing shapes with a particular attribute, students might play versions of *I Spy*. Certain criteria are listed in the sample below, but the attributes can be changed.

Let's all look around.

I am going to say "*I spy . . .*" and you will look for my object.

I spy with my little eye:

- Something that has exactly 3 sides. *OR*
- A 3-D object that is only partly round. *OR*
- A shape with some equal sides. *OR*
- A 3-D shape that has only two identical faces.

➤ Students can also be asked to create shapes with particular attributes. Some samples are given, but, again, substitutions of other attributes can be made. Students can draw or use plasticine or pattern blocks or other premade shapes.

> Make:
>
> - A pentagon that can be cut into a square and a triangle.
> - A pentagon that CANNOT be cut into a square and a triangle.
> - A 3-D shape with 6 faces so that there are no more than 2 that are the same.
> - A 4-sided shape that can be broken into 2 unusual-looking triangles.

➤ Students should have experience cutting shapes into equal parts.

> Choose a circle or a rectangle.
> Cut it into 3 equal pieces in more than one way.

OR

> Cut a rectangle into 8 equal pieces that do not all look the same.

➤ The activity below helps students begin to see that if most of the parts of a whole are colored, then the fraction describing the colored part might be, for example, five-sixths or two-thirds or seven-eighths, but not one-third or one-eighth.

> Choose a circle or a rectangle.
> Cut it into equal pieces.
> Color all but one piece.
> What fraction could be colored?

OR

The activity at the top of the next page is meant to start a foundation for recognizing why it is easier to create arrays for numbers like 12 or 20 or 24 (which have many factors) than for numbers like 5 or 7 or 11 (with few factors). This language is not used yet; this task is simply foundational.

> Which do you find easier:
>   • Cutting a rectangle into 12 equal pieces?
>   • Cutting it into 5 equal pieces?
> Why?

Suggestions for Home Activities: 2nd Grade

You might encourage parents to come to school for a "fun math at home" program or create short videos for them and post them on your school website. Make sure parents are familiar with and comfortable with the kind of math activities in which their children are engaging. You might create a blog with short postings or videos where you model or talk about some of the math activities in which their children are engaging.

There is not a lot of geometry in 2nd grade, but there are a few things parents can do to support their children.

➤ Encourage parents to ask their children to draw shapes of certain types. For example: *I'd love it if you would draw me a shape with a lot of sides and decorate it.* Or: *Can you use the plasticine to make me a shape that has some round and some flat parts?*

➤ Encourage parents to have their child help them partition items, whether food or other things, into halves, thirds, and fourths.

➤ Encourage parents to have their children assist them in partitioning rectangles into rows and columns with equal pieces, and to count the total number of pieces. The rectangle could be a cake or a pan of lasagna being cut into equal pieces, or it could be fabric for a craft project.

➤ It is always valuable to encourage parents to build spatial sense in their children by doing jigsaw puzzles with them or by letting them see simple drawings or shape structures for short periods and asking them to recreate them.

Additional Geometry Activities for 1st and 2nd Grades

These additional geometry activities focus on symmetry, partitioning, and spatial visualization. You might want to add these to the content that the Common Core standards (2010) require. These activities are appropriate for primary grade children and are useful for spatial development.

> Explore what folding or mirror symmetry is with students by folding paper shapes that are symmetric, such as rectangles, squares, circles, regular hexagons, and so forth, on a middle line to create halves. Introduce the word *symmetry*. Explain that one side of the shape is the mirror opposite of the other, but otherwise the two sides are identical.

Look for symmetry in the classroom.

Do more shapes have symmetry or not?

OR

Provide or have students create paper block letters of the alphabet. They can fold to test for symmetry since paper is used.

Which letters of the alphabet are symmetric?

Which are not?

A B C D

OR

To informally introduce the notion of line of symmetry, you could use a task like the one below:

Take a piece of paper. Fold it.

Draw something on one side of the fold that you think looks like half of something.

Cut out your drawing.

Cut through both parts of the paper— the top and the folded part.

Open up the cutout.

What do you see?

> Provide a **transparent mirror** and allow children to see what happens when they use it. The intention is to see that the image "duplicates" the objects. If there are more objects in front of the mirror, there are more "behind" the mirror. Have children lay out a line of objects and see how many objects they see if they move the mirror to the different locations marked in the task at the top of the next page.

Line up four squares or counters like they are shown here.

Move the mirror to each of the lines, one at a time, that are marked.

Each time, how many objects do you see in all?

In your total, include the real objects and what you see in the mirror.

[*Solutions:* 2, 4, 6, 8.]

> You might explore **spatial memory** with students. You could either show a simple geometric visual for a few seconds and get them to draw what they remember, or you could change a drawing or structure and see if they can tell what has changed. Some of the drawings you might show are simple ones like those shown below the activity; others might be created. The important part is discussing how students tried to remember what they saw.

You will see a design for a very short time. Try to remember it.

Try to draw what you remember.

You will get another chance to see it and to change your drawing if you wish.

Possible visuals to remember:

OR

Create a structure with 5–10 blocks. Have the children look at it, but not too long. While the children's eyes are closed (see the activity on the next page), remove, add, or move a block. Once they open their eyes, they will try to recall what the structure used to look like to figure out what changed. You might enjoy reading the book *Changes, Changes* (Hutchins, 1987) with them too.

> Look at the block structure I have created.
>
> Close your eyes while I change it just a little. Open them when I tell you.
>
> Now tell me how the structure changed.

> You could observe whether students notice that two identical objects that are oriented in different ways are identical. When they make the structures for the activity below, they need to recognize if one is really the same as another, just **rotated** or **reflected**.

> Make all the shapes you can using either 4 or 5 linking cubes that are linked together.
>
> Make sure the structures are all different.

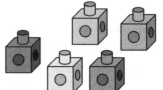

> You could have students consider **perspective**, realizing that two people taking a photo of the same object from different locations will end up with different-looking photos. You could start this discussion by taking a photo of the classroom from two very different spots and asking children to decide where you stood in each case.

> Here are two photos of our classroom.
>
> Do you think I was standing in the same place when I took them?
>
> Where do you think I was standing?

> You could have students develop their ability to predict what objects will look like after they are rotated or reflected. The activity might involve building a simple structure, predicting what it will look like if turned upside down, and then testing.

> Use 5 linking cubes to build a structure.
>
> Without touching the structure, predict what it will look like if you turn it upside down.
>
> Now check your prediction.

OR

The task could be predicting the result of a rotation.

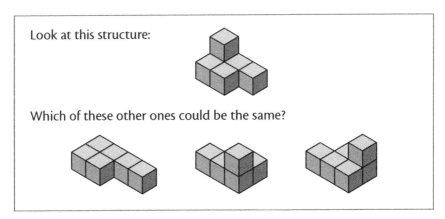

OR

The challenge could be drawing a conclusion about how shapes are being changed and then predicting the result for a new shape. Notice that in this case, all objects were rotated a quarter turn clockwise, but there could have been reflections or half turns or other changes instead.

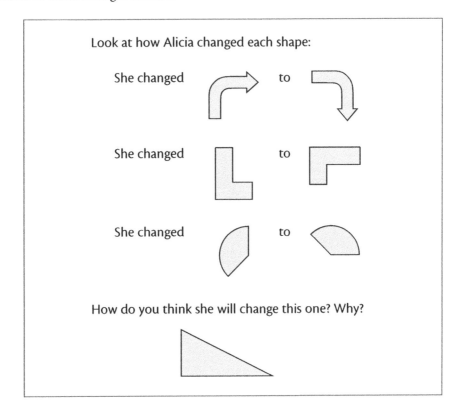

Conclusion

BUILDING a firm foundation in mathematics for young children is a multifaceted challenge for both teachers and parents.

Knowing the fundamentals of math usually makes it much easier for a teacher to provide rich learning activities for students and to know how to address children's unexpected responses.

Knowing the misconceptions students are likely to hold helps a teacher provide appropriate responses when these situations arise.

Having a variety of activities that are designed both to be fun and to build important understandings makes planning instruction easier.

And, finally, having support at home can only help students, especially if parents have been made aware of the kinds of things they can do to promote the development of mathematical understanding in their children.

I hope the materials provided in Chapters 1–6 will make all of this possible for you.

Glossary

1-1 correspondence. When objects in two groups are matched in pairs with one from each group. [Chap. 2, p. 15]

1-dimensional. Having only 1 dimension, such as only length or only width or only height. Objects that are 1-dimensional include lines, line segments, and rays. [Chap. 5, p. 120]

2-dimensional. Having only 2 dimensions, such as only length and width, with no height. A 2-dimensional shape is flat. [Chap. 5, p. 128]

3-dimensional. Having 3 dimensions, such as length, width, and height. A 3-dimensional shape is a concrete object. [Chap. 5, p. 121]

100-chart. A chart with the numbers from 1 to 100 or 0 to 99 displayed in order in 10 rows of 10. [Chap. 4, p. 65]

addend. One of the numbers added together. [Chap. 3, p. 40]

addition and subtraction facts. The 100 combinations of adding two single-digit numbers (0 to 9) together. [Chap. 3, p. 44]

analog clocks. Clocks with faces and hands; normally the numbers 1 to 12 appear on the clock face around a circle. [Chap. 5, p. 131]

apex. The point of a cone. [Chap. 6, p. 179]

associative property (of addition). The number property that suggests that to add three numbers, you can choose whether to group the middle number with the first one first or with the last one first. [Chap. 3, p. 40]

attribute. A feature of an object (e.g., its color or its orientation or a feature like having all equal sides). [Chap. 5, p. 116]

bar diagram. A model that is used to represent the parts that combine to form a whole in addition or subtraction situations; often associated with a teaching method called Singapore math. [Chap. 3, p. 32]

bar graph. A way to show and compare data by using horizontal or vertical bars. [Chap. 5, p. 139]

base. The base of a prism, cone, or cylinder is the face that, in the case of a prism, may or may not be a rectangle and in the case of the cone or cylinder is a circle. [Chap. 6, p. 179]

base-ten blocks. Blocks of different sizes representing place value columns; a larger block is 10 times the size of the next smaller block. Blocks consist of small cubes (1s), rods (10s), and flats (100s). [Chap. 4, p. 73]

benchmark. A familiar measurement or number used for comparing other measurements or as a referent for other numbers (e.g., 1 inch, 1 meter, 10, or 25). [Chap. 4, p. 76]

cardinality. A description of the numerical size of a set of objects. [Chap. 2, p. 7]

circumference. Distance around a rounded object. [Chap. 5, p. 151]

closed (shape). A closed shape results when an area is completely enclosed by lines or curves. [Chap. 6, p. 172]

commutative property (of addition). The number property that suggests that two numbers can be added in either order with the same result. [Chap. 3, p. 39]

compensation. A strategy whereby one or both numbers in a calculation are changed to "friendlier" numbers and then the result is adjusted to compensate for the changes made. [Chap. 3, p. 45]

composition. Combining numbers or shapes to create new numbers or shapes. For example, 10 is composed of two 5s; a rectangle can be composed by combining two squares. [Chap. 3, p. 36]

concrete graph. A graph that uses concrete objects. [Chap. 2, p. 20]

congruent. Exactly the same size and shape. [Chap. 6, p. 176]

conservation of length. A recognition that the length of an object does not change when the object is moved around. [Chap. 5, p. 121]

conservation of number. A recognition that the cardinality or amount does not change when objects are moved around, or whether the objects are replaced by larger ones or not. [Chap. 2, p. 17]

constant difference. A constant difference is maintained in a subtraction when the space between the numbers being subtracted remains unchanged; requires adding or subtracting the same amount to or from both numbers. [Chap. 3, p. 41]

continuous (attribute). A continuous measurement can hold any value 0 or greater. Most measurements, other than counts of discrete objects, are continuous. [Chap. 5, p. 118]

convex. An attribute of a shape when the line segment joining any two points within the shape lies fully within the shape; there are no "dents." [Chap. 6, p. 172]

core. The smallest part of a repeating pattern that repeats. [Chap. 2, p. 16]

counting on. Counting forward but not necessarily starting at 1. [Chap. 2, p. 11]

cross-section. The 2-dimensional shape resulting from cutting through a 3-dimensional shape using a flat plane. [Chap. 6, p. 179]

Cuisenaire rods. A set of 10 colored rods of lengths 1 cm, 2 cm, 3 cm, . . . , 10 cm. [Chap. 2, p. 4]

decomposition. Breaking numbers or shapes into parts. For example, 10 can be decomposed into 4 + 4 + 2; a square can be decomposed into two triangles. [Chap. 3, p. 36]

defining attribute. An attribute that forces a shape to be a certain sort of shape (e.g., a defining attribute for a parallelogram is that there are four straight sides and opposite sides are equal). [Chap. 6, p. 172]

edge. A line segment formed where two faces of a 3-dimensional shape meet. [Chap. 6, p. 177]

ellipse. A rounded shape that looks like an elongated circle. [Chap. 6, p. 172]

equation. A statement using an equals sign where both sides describe the same amount. [Chap. 3, p. 36]

equilateral. A triangle is equilateral if all of its sides and angles are equal. [Chap. 6, p. 169]

face. A flat side of a 3-dimensional shape (e.g., cubes have 6 square faces). [Chap. 6, p. 177]

face map. A way of representing a 3-dimensional shape by showing, individually, each face. [Chap. 6, p. 180]

hexagon. A closed 2-dimensional shape with six straight sides. [Chap. 6, p. 169]

Imperial system. The system of measurement prevalent in the United States; uses units such as inches, feet, yards, miles, ounces, pounds, fluid ounces, quarts, gallons, and so forth. [Chap. 5, p. 121]

isosceles. An attribute of a triangle or trapezoid indicating that two sides are equal. [Chap. 6, p. 169]

iterate. Perform repeatedly. By iterating a unit, we can measure an object. [Chap. 5, p. 119]

line plot. A way to show and compare data that can be sorted into numerical categories; formed by making marks (usually Xs) in a column above positions on the number line. [Chap. 5, p. 136]

line segment. A piece of a line with two endpoints. [Chap. 6, p. 169]

linking cubes. Cubes that can be linked together to create structures. [Chap. 4, p. 71]

metric system. The system of measurement prevalent in many countries in the world; based on units such as the meter and the gram, where units are related by factors of 10. [Chap. 5, p. 121]

missing addend. A form of subtraction where one determines what to add to one number to achieve another. [Chap. 3, p. 34]

multiple. A number that is formed by multiplying a given whole number by another whole number. [Chap. 2, p. 13]

nonstandard unit. A unit of measurement used as the basis for describing other measurements, but one that may vary from person to person (e.g., the length of a pencil or the length of a finger might be used as units for describing length). [Chap. 5, p. 119]

number line. A diagram that shows ordered numbers as points on a line. [Chap. 2, p. 11]

number path. A diagram that shows ordered numbers as connected squares. [Chap. 2, p. 11]

numeral. A symbol used to represent a quantity (e.g., the numeral for eight is 8). [Chap. 2, p. 16]

obtuse angle. An angle with a measure between 90° and 180°. [Chap. 6, p. 169]

open number line. A number line where not all numbers are premarked and the user chooses which numbers are shown. [Chap. 4, p. 80]

pan balance. A device for weighing with two pans and a balanced beam. It remains level when items on both sides are equal in weight, and it tips toward the side with the heavier item otherwise. [Chap. 5, p. 119]

parallel. A feature of a pair of lines or planes that indicates they will never meet, even if extended. [Chap. 6, p. 172]

parallelogram. A quadrilateral with opposite sides that are parallel. [Chap. 6, p. 169]

partition. Cut into pieces, or decompose. [Chap. 6, p. 168]

pattern blocks. A set of shapes that includes hexagons, trapezoids, squares, parallelograms, and triangles of particular sizes. [Chap. 3, p. 65]

pentagon. A closed 2-dimensional shape with five straight sides. [Chap. 6, p. 169]

perspective. A point of view. [Chap. 6, p. 196]

picture graph. A graph that uses pictures to represent quantities. [Chap. 5, p. 138]

place value. A system for writing numbers where a digit's placement in a numeral reflects its value; in our case, a 10-for-1 trading system involving ones, tens, hundreds, and so forth is used. [Chap. 3, p. 43]

place value chart. A chart showing columns of ones, tens, hundreds, and so forth. [Chap. 4, p. 74]

plane. A flat surface that extends infinitely far in two directions. [Chap. 6, p. 169]

positional vocabulary. Words or phrases used to describe how two objects are positioned relative to one another (e.g., far, near, above, below). [Chap. 6, p. 168]

proportional reasoning. The capacity to think of a group of objects as a single object; the capacity to think of one amount as a set of another amount. [Chap. 5, p. 154]

quadrilateral. A closed 2-dimensional shape with four straight sides. [Chap. 6, p. 169]

ray. A piece of a line with one endpoint. [Chap. 6, p. 169]

rectangular prism. A 3-dimensional shape with 6 rectangular faces; opposite faces are congruent. [Chap. 6, p. 177]

reflect. Use a mirror to see an "opposite" image. [Chap. 6, p. 196]

rekenrek. A frame of beads, featuring 2 or 10 rows, each with 10 beads organized by color into two groups of 5, each group a different color. [Chap. 2, p. 12]

right angle. An angle measuring 90°. [Chap. 6, p. 172]

rotate. Turn an object leaving some point fixed. [Chap. 6, p. 196]

scale. The amount that one unit in a graph represents. [Chap. 5, p. 138]

skeleton. A representation of a 3-dimensional object that shows only its edges and vertices; often created with straws representing edges and small balls of clay as its vertices. [Chap. 6, p. 179]

skip count. Count in a patterned way that skips particular numbers (e.g., counting by 10s skips any number that does not end in 0; counting by 5s skips any number not ending in 5 or 0, etc.). [Chap. 2, p. 8]

sorting rule. A description of how it is determined which items of a group go together. [Chap. 5, p. 134]

spatial memory. A part of human memory associated with information about spatial orientation and positioning. [Chap. 6, p. 195]

spatial reasoning. An ability to think about objects in 3 dimensions and draw conclusions about those objects. [Chap. 5, p. 154]

spatial relationships. A specification of how some object is located in the environment (in space) relative to some referent. [Chap. 6, p. 167]

square corner. An angle of 90° formed at the vertex of a shape. [Chap. 6, p. 172]

standard unit. An unambiguous measurement based on units that hold the same meaning for everyone (e.g., inch, yard, meter). [Chap. 5, p. 119]

subitizing. Recognizing an amount by just looking and not counting. [Chap. 2, p. 11]

symmetry (reflective). An attribute of a shape where one half is the mirror image of the other. [Chap. 6, p. 172]

tally marks. A system of sticks or marks, grouped in 5s, used to keep track of items. [Chap. 2, p. 12]

ten-frame. A model with 10 cells organized in 2 rows of 5 columns. [Chap. 2, p. 12]

trajectory. A path (e.g., a path of learning). [Chap. 2, p. 10]

transparent mirror. A mirror that can be seen through; with this type of mirror, a student can draw the image of an object that is viewed in it. [Chap. 6, p. 194]

trapezoid. A quadrilateral with one pair of parallel sides. [Chap. 6, p. 169]

triangle. A closed shape with three straight sides. [Chap. 6, p. 169]

unifix cubes. Cubes that can be linked to others in only one way. [Chap. 4, p. 71]

unit (of measurement). A measurement used as the basis for describing other measurements (e.g., 1 inch is a unit of length). [Chap. 5, p. 116]

unitizing. A strategy where groups of items are thought of as singular objects. [Chap. 4, p. 71]

Venn diagram. A sorting diagram using closed shapes in which to place sorted items. [Chap. 5, p. 135]

vertex. A corner of a shape; the plural is *vertices*. [Chap. 6, p. 170]

volume. The amount of material required to create an object; measure of the "size" in 3 dimensions of a 3-dimensional object. [Chap. 5, p. 130]

References

Allen, P. (1982). *Who sank the boat?* New York, NY: The Putnam & Grosset Group.

Baxter, N. (1994). *The enormous turnip.* London, UK: Ladybird Books.

Bay-Williams, J. M., & Van de Walle, J. A. (2010). *Field experience guide: Resources for teachers of elementary and middle school mathematics.* Boston, MA: Allyn and Bacon.

Boaler, J. (2014). Research suggests that timed tests cause math anxiety. *Teaching Children Mathematics, 20,* 469–473.

Bogart, J. E. (1989). *Ten for dinner.* Toronto, ON: Scholastic.

Box Cars and One-Eyed Jacks. (2015). *Shuffling into math with fun family games.* Available at https://www.boxcarsandoneeyedjacks.com/product/shuffling-into-math-with-fun -family-games/

Breyfogle, M. L., & Williams, L. E. (2008). Designing and implementing worthwhile tasks. *Teaching Children Mathematics, 15,* 276–280.

Carle, E. (1994). *The very hungry caterpillar.* New York, NY: Philomel Books.

Carle, E. (1996a). *The grouchy ladybug.* New York, NY: HarperCollins.

Carle, E. (1996b). *1, 2, 3, to the zoo: A counting book.* New York, NY: Philomel Books.

Caswell, B. (2013). *The math for young children (M_4YC) project: A no ceiling approach to math learning in an urban school.* Toronto, ON: Centre for Urban Schooling—OISE. Available at http://cus.oise.utoronto.ca/UserFiles/File/CUS-Caswell_research_brief.pdf

Clements, D. H. (2004). Major themes and recommendations. In D. H. Clements, J. Sarama, & A. DiBiase (Eds.), *Engaging young children in mathematics: Standards for early childhood mathematics education* (pp. 7–72). Mahwah, NJ: Lawrence Erlbaum Associates.

Clements, D., & Sarama, J. (2011). *Learning trajectories for primary grades mathematics.* Available at http://ncscdfoundationsofmathematics.ncdpi.wikispaces.net/file/view/ Building+Block+Learning+Trajectories.pdf

Common Core State Standards Initiative. (2010). *Common Core State Standards for Mathematics.* Available at http://www.corestandards.org/assets/CCSSI_Math%20Standards .pdf

Cooper, M. (2011). *Meet the teens.* Mustang, OK: Tate Publishing.

Crews, D. (1992). *Ten black dots.* Toronto, ON: Scholastic.

Dahl, M. (2006). *Toasty toes: Counting by tens.* North Mankato, MN: Picture Window Books.

Danielson, C. (2017). *Which one doesn't belong? A shapes book.* Portland, ME: Stenhouse.

Duke, K. (2000). *Twenty is too many.* New York, NY: Dutton Children's Books.

Duke, K. (2001). *One guinea pig is not enough.* New York, NY: Puffin Books.

Gelman, R., & Gallistel, C. R. (1978). *The child's understanding of number.* Cambridge, MA: Harvard University Press.

Gerth, M. (2000). *Ten little lady bugs.* Atlanta, GA: Piggy Toes Press.

Godfrey, L., & O'Connor, M. C. (1995). The vertical hand span: Nonstandard units, expressions and symbols in the classroom. *Journal of Mathematical Behavior, 14,* 327–345.

Gray, E. (2003). *Track pack: Animal tracks in full life size.* Mechanicsburg, PA: Stackpole Books.

Harris, T. (2009). *The clock struck one.* Minneapolis, MN: Milbrook Press.

Hoban, T. (1996). *Shapes, shapes, shapes.* New York, NY: Greenwillow Books.

Hufferd-Ackles, K., Fuson, K. C., & Sherin, M. G. (2004). Describing levels and components of a math-talk learning community. *Journal for Research in Mathematics Education, 35*(2), 81–116.

Hutchins, P. (1987). *Changes, changes.* New York, NY: Simon & Schuster.

Jenkins, S. (2011). *Actual size.* Boston, MA: Houghton Mifflin.

Learn Alberta. (2007). *Posing worthwhile mathematical tasks.* Available at http://www.learn alberta.ca/content/mewa/html/other/posingworthwhile.html

Long, L. (1996). *Domino addition.* Watertown, MA: Charlesbridge.

Mandler, G., & Shebo, B. J. (1982). Subitizing: An analysis of its component processes. *Journal of Experimental Psychology: General, 111*(1982): 1–22.

Murphy, S. (2000). *Monster musical chair.* New York, NY: HarperCollins.

Murphy, S. (2005). *It's about time!* New York, NY: HarperCollins.

Nagel, K. (2009). *Shapes that roll.* Maplewood, NJ: Blue Apple Books.

National Council for Curriculum and Assessment (NCCA). (2009). *Aistear: The early childhood curriculum framework.* Dublin, Ireland: Author.

National Research Council. (2001). *Adding it up: Helping children learn mathematics.* J. Kilpatrick, J. Swafford, & B. Findell (Eds.). Mathematics Learning Study Committee, Center for Education, Division of Behavioral and Social Sciences and Education. Washington, DC: National Academy Press.

Piaget, J. (1965). *The child's conception of number.* New York, NY: W. W. Norton.

Scarry, R. (1968). *Richard Scarry's best counting book ever.* New York, NY: HarperCollins.

Sierra, J. (2007). *What time is it, Mr. Crocodile?* San Diego, CA: Harcourt Books.

Sinclair, N. (2014). *Touchcounts.* Available at http://touchcounts.ca

Starkey, P., & Cooper, R. G., Jr. (1995). The development of subitizing in young children. *British Journal of Developmental Psychology, 13*(4), 399–420.

Szilagyi, J., Clements, D. H., & Sarama, J. (2013). Young children's understandings of length measurement: Evaluating a learning trajectory. *Journal for Research in Mathematics Education, 44,* 581–620.

Teppo, A. (1991). Van Hiele levels of geometric thought revisited. *Mathematics Teacher, 84,* 210–221.

Walsh, E. S. (1991). *Mouse count.* San Diego, CA: Harcourt Children's Books.

Walsh, E. S. (2007). *Mouse shapes.* San Diego, CA: Harcourt Children's Books.

Wolf, N. B. (2015). *Modeling with mathematics.* Portsmouth, NH: Heinemann.

Index

This index covers instructional concepts and topics; the names of authors, book titles, and songs cited in the text are also included. Mathematical terminology is not indexed in detail. However, the Glossary (pages 201–206) lists the primary mathematical terms featured in the text and activities. Each Glossary entry ends with a chapter and page designator identifying the location of the first occurrence of the term.

About the Author

MARIAN SMALL is the former dean of education at the University of New Brunswick. She speaks regularly about K–12 mathematics instruction.

She has been an author on many mathematics text series at both the elementary and the secondary levels. She has served on the author team for the National Council of Teachers of Mathematics (NCTM) Navigation series (pre-K–2), as the NCTM representative on the Mathcounts question writing committee for middle school mathematics competitions throughout the United States, and as a member of the editorial panel for the NCTM 2011 yearbook on motivation and disposition.

Dr. Small is probably best known for her books *Good Questions: Great Ways to Differentiate Mathematics Instruction* and *More Good Questions: Great Ways to Differentiate Secondary Mathematics Instruction* (with Amy Lin). *Eyes on Math: A Visual Approach to Teaching Math Concepts* was published in 2013, as was *Uncomplicating Fractions to Meet Common Core Standards in Math, K–7*. She authored *Uncomplicating Algebra to Meet Common Core Standards in Math, K–8* in 2014 and *Teaching Mathematical Thinking: Tasks and Questions to Strengthen Practices and Processes* in 2017. She is also author of the three editions of a text for university preservice teachers and practicing teachers, *Making Math Meaningful to Canadian Students: K–8*, as well as the professional resources *Big Ideas from Dr. Small: Grades 4–8*; *Big Ideas from Dr. Small: Grades K–3*; and *Leaps and Bounds toward Math Understanding: Grades 3–4, Grades 5–6,* and *Grades 7–8*, all published by Nelson Education Ltd. More recently, she has authored a number of additional resources focused on open questions, including *Open Questions for the Three-Part Lesson, K–3: Numeration and Number Sense*; *Open Questions for the Three-Part Lesson, K–3: Measurement and Pattern and Algebra*; *Open Questions for the Three-Part Lesson, 4–8: Numeration and Number Sense*; and *Open Questions for the Three-Part Lesson, 4–8: Measurement and Pattern and Algebra,* all published by Rubicon Publishing. She has created a digital resource, *MathUp,* with Rubicon Publishing, for providing rich instruction for Grades 1–6 and a soon-to-be-released resource, published by ASCD, *The School Leader's Guide to Building and Sustaining Math Success* (with Doug Duff), to help principals improve math instruction in their schools.

She also led the research resulting in the creation of maps describing student mathematical development in each of the five NCTM mathematical strands for the K–8 levels and has created the associated professional development program, PRIME.

Printed and bound by CPI Group (UK) Ltd, Croydon, CR0 4YY

09/06/2025

14685981-0002